CAPRICORN HOROSCOPE 2023

Your essential guide to love, money, happiness and using moon magic!

Hi guys,

A warm welcome to all my regular readers and a special hello to all new readers. I aim to provide a comprehensive insight into 2023 with spiritual, psychological insight, and down to earth common sense advice.

Every year when I write these books I just cannot believe how fast the year has gone, and that it's once again time to write and publish the series for the next year.

As many of you know, I've been producing these books since 2014, and boy has the world changed since then and 2023 will be a year of unprecedented change in world terms, that's why I've decided to also do an Astrology book of World predictions which include predictions for countries and certain leaders, because I feel that we need to be forwarded and for armed.

It's important to remember that no matter what is happening in the outside world, we all have our lives to live and karma to resolve and we must enjoy our own unique journey. Remember, we are all meant to be here at this very time, to experience what we are experiencing and we should never underestimate our own power and ability to thrive and make a difference.

Yes, we are all at different points along our own personal journey, but what I want to do with these books is encourage you all to understand your own creativity, power and never to underestimate yourself, to feel lost all to lose a sense of purpose. We are all here for a reason and we all have a valuable contribution to make in different ways, and hopefully my annual books have inspired you to understand your purpose and connect with some inspiration.

Fortunately the Saturn Square Uranus that was happening between Saturn in Aquarius and Uranus in Taurus is now done and dusted, which is a good thing because that was creating an enormous amount of tension within all of us, because the energies of Saturn and Uranus are so different. However, what we have coming this year is Pluto moving into Aquarius, and every time Pluto has changed signs there have been dramatic events worldwide that have changed history: it could be the birth of new countries, technological changes, conflict, economic shifts, innovations and the advent of new philosophies or political systems. So we should all be ready to embrace change with an open mind and we should remember not to be overly concerned with things that we are not able to change, because what we all can change is our attitude and it's always better to be optimistic and proactive.

I've often seen in my career as an astrologer that astrology works best for people who make plans, who act on those plans, who motivate themselves and who don't wait around for things to happen. Good things happen when we take chances, when we get up and seize opportunities or even just envisage then, very little happens we stick to comfort zones, resist change and hang onto the past for dear life, irrespective of the planets.

I always believe that it's important to understand our roots, to know where we come from and how our experiences have shaped us and given us wisdom. Our cumulative heritage is always important, but we can't live in the past, things are changing and we have to keep moving along and adapting, and using our wits and innate dynamic energy to thrive.

Love Lisa

This is a very exciting year for Capricorn as the planet Pluto, which is the slowest moving and often the most turbulent, passionate and disruptive of planets, is finally leaving Capricorn as it enters Aquarius. This is an important moment for Capricorn, it's a time for reflection and also a time to contemplate a new era dawning in your life. So this is an excellent year but you do need to come to terms work with what has happened in the past 14 years, it's time to settle any karmic debts, it's a time for forgiveness, burying the hatchet and for conclusively dealing with any lingering resentment from the previous 14 years.

2023 is a time for you to reflect on the successes of the last 14 years and how you can now take that forward into a new chapter in your life, a chapter where you are more mature, more self-confident and an awful lot wiser

Just as sometimes at the beginning of a new term at school or college, we need to recap what was learned in the previous term, it's well worth your while thinking about the experiences gained and the important life lessons you've learnt in the last 14 years. You do need to make a mental note of these just so that you can cement them into your mind, because these are going to be valuable during particularly the next five years as you move forward.

So this is a wonderful phase for regeneration, for renewal, for making a new start and often for a complete metamorphosis. So if you have been wanting to radically alter the way you are perceived, the way you go about your life, your mindset etc. this is the perfect time to do it.

With Jupiter in Aries and later in the year in Taurus, this is a fantastic time for family life, big family events and family celebrations and it's also a wonderful time for new romance and creativity. So there's an awful lot to look forward to, it's a busy year and one which is set to be quite important in terms of the next decade of your life.

Family Fortunes are in the up

Jupiter in Aries from the beginning of this year marks an important time for family life, this is quite an expansive, positive time and there may be good news for the family in terms of new arrivals. However, it is also a time to make peace with the past and to settle differences with family members, so this is a key opportunity to mend what's broken and to make amends in the most private sphere of your life.

It's very important for you to restore relations with family members, not because you can necessarily be best buddies with them, but from a point of view of your own psychological healing you need to put certain things to rest. You need to absolve yourself from any guilt you may have had stemming from your own behaviour and you need to be able to forgive, and then to release the situation. You shouldn't be overly concerned with the actions of the other person, they will either be happy to accept an olive branch, but even if they aren't, at least you can feel you have settled the bad karma from your perspective.

Big Celebrations

This can be a great year to plan a big family event and its perfect if you have any family members getting married, are getting married yourself or if someone has a big anniversary coming. It's a great time to have large family gatherings, to connect with people you haven't seen and in some cases you may make a long journey to see family that you haven't seen for many years. It's a time of coming together and reveling in old bonds.

Back to your roots

This year you have a renewed interest in your family tree and your family ancestry, and certainly chatting to older family members or drawing on their wisdom is a feature. Being more involved with the older generation of the family in order to help them in practical ways, but also to draw on their knowledge of the family history can be something that is very rewarding and ends up having quite a profound effect on you.

It's certainly a year where getting a stronger sense of your roots can help you to get a better grip of who you are and that can help you to be more positive in life, and also in your relationships. They often say that even a small wind can blow over a tree with no roots, and conversely some of the largest trees have networks of roots that are almost a mile wide, and in 2023 you have to think of yourself as one of those wonderful large trees and therefore you should be spreading your roots as deep as possible. This means increasing the strength of family bonds, maybe becoming reacquainted with your culture or just understanding better when you come from.

So while this is a great year for future planning, often you need to know where you coms from first, you need a clearer sense of your heritage and you need to come to terms with your past and then you can make much better decisions about what you need to be happy in the future, from relationships and career.

Shifting the dial of consciousness

With a little bit of effort and positivity, problems within your family or your life can often be cleared up, usually because there's a shift in consciousness or new information comes to light which can help you straighten things out. It's important for you to be warm and generous in your emotions, you don't have to be effusive, but you certainly must use this year to be more demonstrative and tactile to family members and to show you care in a variety of ways, not just as a provider.

The Elders

If you have a good relationship with your parents, that should be even more supportive in sustaining you and giving you good advice, and even if the relationship has been bad in the past there's no reason you can't improve it, and you should work very hard at improving your relationship with your parents. If your parents have passed on, forgiving them and making peace with their memory is important, because this will help make your family life more successful, and your personal life more secure than ever before.

Gold in your backyard

This is certainly a year when you must invest in your family life, the more
you invests in the people who mean most you - these can be family but
also friends, neighbors or your personal support networks - the more you
can draw on a sense of belonging, and these people will reciprocate with
support years down the line.

If you have been unhappy, or have faced quite a lot of psychological crises
in the last few years, or have had many difficult pills to swallow at a
psychological level, this year can really help increase your inner sense of
calm and contentment. You can get a lot more in touch with your inner
self, and it's a time when it's easier for you to handle truths and facts that
you're normally reluctant to face, and this can help settle you down
emotionally, and is very helpful in restoring relationships and easing
decision-making as with you go into the second half of the year.

Swinging singles

What's great about 2023 is that it is excellent for romance and dating, so if
you are single, this is a perfect time to be more active on the social scene,
to join a dating app, or to start doing a new sport with a view to potentially
meeting someone who is a like-minded.

You tend to have an adventurous, positive spirit and the idea in love this
year is to take a 'nothing ventured nothing gained attitude', you shouldn't be
looking to get cozy or settle down quite quickly, you should be looking to
play the field, see what's available, experiment with different types of
personalities whom you may have dismissed out of hand before, and see
how that makes you feel.

Love should be embraced with a spirit of adventure within you, so you
don't want to go into dating with a very conservative, closed-minded
attitude, you want to consider all possibilities and give everyone a fair
chance.

This can be a good year to meet a fellow partner while travelling, but
sports is another good way too, or through a creative interest.

Children are the future

The area of children in general is favored this year, so there are a couple of possibilities: if you've older you may become a grandparent; if you're younger you may consider having children; or if you meet a new partner, you may get on very well with their children, which helps facilitate the relationship.

In general, your relationship with your own children or your step children can improve this year, and even if things have been difficult before, there's a great chance to turn over a new leaf and develop new more positive attitudes to the relationship. However, you must remember to be hands off, this is not a time when being controlling, authoritarian or over fussy works with children, you have to learn to trust their judgement and to show them that you believe in them.

In some cases, children can be quite expensive this year, but on the other hand you want to foster their development, and you want to get quite involved in helping them to achieve their dreams. So if you can pay for extra music lessons, sports training or such like to help them that is what you're prepared to do.

Creative Explosion

This is a terrific year for your creative projects, so whether you are pursuing creativity for a living or in connection with your hobbies, you're certainly inspired and it can be quite exciting for you developing ideas and taking them through to a conclusion.

You're very inventive and great at problem solving, particularly in the second half of the year, and this can lend itself to creative development of technological products, or finding innovative solutions, so you are quite inventive and you can use that in management, IT or science careers.

It's Positivity Plus

You tend to have a lot of energy and a positive attitude, and this can make you a very motivational force, therefore it's excellent for working with youth or children in sports development or creative development. So this is excellent for all Capricorn are following careers as sports instructors, teachers or who work with young people.

Hotting up through the Summer

The second half of the year tends to be filled with activity, both social activity and work-related matters, but all of these have quite a fun overtone, particularly because you are leading and exercising lot of self-expression and thus you are more able to use your ideas in ways that helps you to develop self-esteem and self-confidence.

Love is Allegro

While new love affairs can develop quickly, often the friendship and the fun factor is the most important element of love this year, but what's not to be missed is the fact that new relationships can help your own personal development and can go a long way to enhance your self-confidence and self-esteem. So no matter what happens in relationships this year, some may go onto marriage, some may go onto just being lifelong friends, but whichever way, they have a healing and therapeutic effect on your soul, and as I say help improve your self-worth and self-confidence.

Reconnecting with your passions

This year it's important for Capricorn to connect with your creative spirit, and in doing that you will rediscover your strength and determination, but also your power potential to change your life.

Capricorn is very creative, you've stylish, you have a good sense of color and proportion which means that you are actually very talented in artistic fields, however because you very often pursue a traditional route in terms of your career and you look for stability, you can neglect your more creative and artistic side, but this is an excellent year for you to start exploring that facet of yourself.

Opening the channels

Capricorn inevitably feels the need to be responsible and to take ownership of situations, however you often fail to properly express all of your emotions, but this can lead to a lot of pent-up frustration and a lot of internal blockages in your energy field.

2022 is a fantastic time for you to do any work on chakras in terms of releasing blockages in energy and creating a free flow of vitality throughout your body. So if you have been having any health issues, or have been feeling rather depleted or tired, a great way to tackle this is through working with your chakra energy, with a practitioner, or learning more about rebalancing chakras through mind power.

The artistic prerogative

Another great outlet for you, is exploring your passions through creativity. Because you usually feel an inability to express yourself authentically, as you are concerned for your reputation, or for maintaining a sense of calm and harmony, but creativity can be an excellent way for you to express your more volatile and colorful emotions in a way that's not going to upset others.

Dynamite in a laser beam

This is a year when you have a lot of stamina and your underlying patience and inner calm are emphasized, making it more easy for you to stay focused on all the important goals that you have without missing a trick.

In terms of your work and your social goals, this is an excellent period because you can connect to both your inner and outer strength, you have increasing confidence and you present to other people as strong and charismatic.

While Capricorn has quite a powerful yet persevering personality, if you've had a lot of self-doubt, this is a year where your confidence shines through and you feels able to tackle those doubts head on, and often some impulsive rather sporadic behaviour can help you to do that.

Roar

In terms of your married life, it's important for you to take a compassionate approach, but in the bedroom you need to be a ferocious lion who seeks to be tamed by your partner. So while in polite company it's important for you to show a patient and affectionate approach, in the bedroom it's time for you to sling off the reins in terms of your sex life and to be far more assertive and flamboyant.

A taste for your talents

Capricorn wants to achieve self-mastery, it is very important for you to have a degree of self-control and to make the best use of all your talents, but you often neglect the talents and aspects of your personality which are a little bit more outrageous, controversial and impetuous. So it's time for you to get in touch with the child within, and be reminded of your passionate instinctual side which should be allowed to burst out frequently this year. While you want to be compassionate to others, you don't want to be too tame.

Getting into the groove

If you have felt worn down or stressed out, things are going to get better. This is an excellent time for healing and recuperation, but you should not neglect the power of your own mind because optimism and positive thinking is vital to improvements in your overall health and well-being. As I said when I talked about balancing your chakras, you need to be a very aware of negative energy whether it's coming from thought patterns or from situations in your life, and you want to be addressing that and tackling that toxic energy.

A certain amount of patience and finesse is needed this year, so once again it's striking a balance between some daring and courageous activity, with determined and tenacious follow-through.

The right stuff

You need to cultivate the belief that you are on the right path, that you know what you're doing and that everything is working together for good. Overall this is an incredibly positive year as fate and karma should be working together to push you in the right direction, and you have a chance to excel. Whatever you are battling with, you will overcome, as long as you develop a thoroughly positive attitude and stay focused on ever improving inner and outer strength.

There's often a good news financially this year, and in terms of money and your creative projects, you can have a fair bit of luck. Often this year things suddenly go your way even if unexpectedly, so it's a year when you can really count your blessings.

New health kicks

This year Mars is spending the first 3 months of the year in Gemini, which equates to your solar sixth house. This is an excellent time for you to reform your diet and implement new health and fitness regimes. This represents more energy and motivation when it comes to improving health, fitness and losing weight, so these are key aims that you should address. The first part of the year is also about competition, so you may be thinking of signing up for a marathon or triathlon so you have a concrete goal to focus on working towards.

There is a warning however, as Mars in the 6th can lead to increased problems with inflammation, so if you do have any inflammatory health issues, you need to be thinking of food supplements and alkaline diets, or a change of lifestyle to address inflammation and body acidity, because these are definitely problem areas.

While you should certainly be active physically during the first part of the year, you must also be careful to warm up properly and to support your body for fitness in all the right ways. You don't want to be rushing headlong into ill-advised fitness regimes that aren't suitable for your state of health.

Super-efficient

You've going to hit the ground running in terms of work, the beginning of the year is an excellent time for organizing, becoming more efficient etc. so you may want to work at recruiting new staff, maybe outsourcing some of your work or introducing new equipment or new manufacturing techniques to help you complete your work more quickly.

You enjoy playing with engines, tinkering with technical things and you've very mechanically minded, and thus the first part of the year is excellent for fixing things. So whether you works in a career where you work with tools and machinery, or does it as a hobby, that can be a fantastic outlet, as you enjoy this a lot.

Fire and desire

During this year you have to recognize all aspects of your desire nature: your desire for security, material well-being and love, but also your more animal, carnal desires. It's a time where it's ok for you to feel passionate, impatient and to have lower impulse control. It's a time when you need to incorporate more of your instinctual reactions and bring them into balance with your more patient conservative side. The Capricorn in you likes to take your time, likes to be sure and doesn't like to rush in, but there's a certain part of you this year that wants to be more adventurous more outrageous, and to live life in a more spontaneous way.

This means that this is a year where you have to take a few chances, take a few risks etc., but you don't need to act out of rage or in anger, but you certainly want to act from your heart without tempering everything by what your head has to say.

Getting your house in order

The fourth house is a very private and personal sphere and with Jupiter in your solar fourth house for approximately the first six months of the year, this is much better suited to getting your house in order. Thus you may want to do things like sort out your pension, deal with property matters and any activities like house-hunting, moving home or renovations, as these are quite ideal for the first part of the year. This can be a good year for you to improve your home, to make better use of a home office or to improve the welfare of the entire family.

There's a theme of expansion, so you might need to increase the capacity of your home for a new family member or for family coming to stay.

Lying in wait

In terms of your career, this is a key preparation time, it's excellent for research, for writing projects and for generally just preparing. So you don't want to particularly launch into anything new, do any grand public relations projects, implement new management ideas or apply for new jobs. In the first part of the year, you must fully understand what you want, how you are going to go about it and gather all the information you need.

This is a perfect year for Capricorns who are interested in writing about history, culture, creative writing and also researching in general, because you can be extremely productive and you should find information that is very helpful.

Looking into your soul

Capricorn must also experience an inner sense of knowing, you need to draw strength from remembering how you have endured and overcome all the obstacles that life has thrown upon you, and you need to reflect about how much inner strength you actually have, and then you must project that out in more confident way.

Capricorn often lacks confidence and that can lead to you being a little bit cautious and conservative in romance, but this year you need to throw everything at love and romance and embrace it in ways like never before, and the way to do that is via strength and your confidence. To improve your confidence, you need to be less modest and spend more time focusing on your achievements and everything you have overcome in life.

Argy bargy

You do have to watch out for conflict with colleagues, as often in the first part of the year you are impatient and you want to get things done, and thus you may perceive other people as impeding you or getting in your way.

Yu work best when you have projects that you can excel at without relying on others, you don't particularly enjoy team work. At the beginning of the year you want to get on with it and make a difference, and you get very frustrated with people who don't pull their weight. Alternatively, if you want to lead by example, you could be the one in the office that gets everyone else motivated and up for it.

Financial matters

With Leo retrograde during the summer months in your solar eighth house, this is an excellent time for you to work on your financial affairs. You may want to devise new tax saving plans and processes in your business like audit, accounting and bookkeeping should be reviewed, updated or possibly changed so that you can be more efficient.

The middle part of the year will also be a time in relationships where you have to have more important and serious discussions with your partner, particularly about financial issues, but there may also be emotional issues that have to be resolved. The summer months in the Northern Hemisphere are a time when you may need to deal alone, or with your partner, with an ex or your partner's ex. Something from the past could crop up which is troublesome, and that may open old scars, but it has to be dealt with.

You should be careful in the summer months of taking on new obligations in terms of loans and debt, because these could end up being quite onerous and not exactly what you were expecting, or you may feel you've been led down the garden path.

Money matters during this phase need a lot of patience, persistence and a wise head, you should also choose your advisers with care, and develop better relationships with your accountant or tax advisor so that you feel you can have more confidence in their advice.

Essence and Energies – "When there's no one else
Look inside yourself
Like your oldest friend
Just trust the voice within
Then you'll find the strength"

The essence of this month is your ability to improve yourself via self-control. Capricorn are an extremely determined, gutsy sign and this month I want you to connect with that inner steely grit that you have.

This is a month where I want you to think about all the imperfections in your life and your character, and I want you to pick something about your life that you want to work on and totally reshape. This may be a physical goal, like weight loss, or something to improve your appearance and outer health, or anything that you been wanting to do for a long time. Alternatively it may be an aspect of your character that you want to improve on.

Capricorn as a sign can be quite serious and this often leads to a little bit of pessimism. Even though you are highly pragmatic, your cautious nature means that you are often predisposed to err on the side of the glass being half empty, and there's nothing wrong with that as there is space for all different personalities, however this month I want you to take a deep breath every time you want to criticize yourself or entertain feelings of rejection, loneliness and isolation. Then I want you to fill that gap by consciously affirming that you believe in yourself, you love yourself and you are fabulous. There's no need to be modest, it's a time for you to thoroughly appreciate yourself and give yourself positive encouraging messages no matter what is going on!

Affirmation: "I use my determination and gritty character to change my mindsets and conscious state for the better, I'm positive about myself and my personality."

Love and Romance

This is quite a good time of year for Capricorn to meet new partners, you're a lot more flirtatious and you may join dating apps. You quite like chatting to different people online and getting a feel for what's out there. However you're quite experimental and you're looking for your ego to be stimulated rather than to immediately jump into a very intense relationship.

You have a sense that this year is going to be quite important and there will be a lot happening, and therefore you want to keep your options open, so it's unlikely that you will want to have more than a few dates with one person this month, simply because you are so busy. However, you also lack the necessary appetite for affection and physical relationships, whereas you rather enjoy communication, a little bit of banter and having your curiosity piqued.

Career and Aspiration

This month the most important word is action, you must avoid procrastination. The beginning of the year is an excellent time for doing the groundwork, for moving aside obstacles and rejecting anything that you believe will stop you from attaining what you want to achieve this year. It's very important for you to start the year with a lot of focus and determination, and therefore things like action plans and strategies are really important because you must be systematic and methodical.

I think you may feel like you have to take a deep breath and steel yourself, it's time for you to be resourceful and it's often best start with the most difficult problems first and then forward that way.

You have an excellent ability to analyze and understand detail, and even with complex problems, you have a tenacity to work through them.

This is an excellent month to get noticed within your career, it's a good time to impress those in authority. So this is not a month to be extremely controversial, to look to step on anyone's toes or to rock the boat. It is a time however when hard work, diplomacy and your PR ability is definitely noticed.

For those of you who are looking for careers in a profession or looking to advance in your profession, this is a very good month so you should speak to your boss about opportunities to progress in your career, or you should be filling out job applications or making yourself visible to potential employees on social media, because it's highly likely right now that your skills are in high demand and you can gain a fantastic new position, albeit something quite traditional.

Adventure and Motivation

This can be an exciting month for a staycation, you and your partner may take a short break in order to explore more of the history or culture of your own country, or just get away somewhere to the great outdoors to experience nature and to get some vigorous exercise.

This is also quite a fun time to start thinking about home improvement projects and things that you and your partner would like to achieve to make your home more welcoming to visitors, or more conducive to your aspirations for your family or your home office.

This can be quite an exciting time for house hunting and looking for suitable new places to stay.

This is definitely a month to face your fears. Often fears become obstacles simply because we keep pushing them to the back of our mind, but when we do that we are actually reinforcing a notion in our heads that we can't deal with these things. However once you deal with a problem or any crisis in your life, even if you only do it in a piecemeal way by taking a small step, you immediately send your higher self a message that you are taking action and being assertive in this matter, and this can be the difference between turning something around or sitting bogged down worrying about something.

Marriage and Family

Capricorn can be quite evasive in relationships, however after Mercury goes direct on the 19th, you are more willing to have discussions with your partner in a more productive way.

However, Capricorn is not always forthcoming and you can be a little bit tricky to put down this month, it's hard to get a straight answer out of you and at some stage it may feel that you are making excuses or trying to pass the buck.

Capricorn is very non-confrontational in January, you are in the mood for being more relaxed and especially in relationships you are looking for easy answers, as you want to avoid anything too emotionally draining. That's why you don't want to have any deep conversations or broach any contentious subjects, you kinda just wants a laid-back start to the year in terms of relationships.

During this month it can feel like a long cruise rather than an international flight, and what I mean by that is progress is slow, so whatever you and your partner are tackling, whether you are trying to increase romance, deal with financial issues or family problems, it takes a lot of patience and persistence.

However, often what is at the root of things going so slowly is a highly rigid approach. You and your partner are probably feeling stuck in a rut, and although there's a degree of frustration and even impatience for things to change, there's actually a lack of willingness on either of your parts to take bold steps, and take a few risks in making that change.

So the key now as a couple is having an innovative approach to the way you do things, taking something that you've always done and just turning it on its head, turning it upside down and looking at it a different way. Often being really grounded and rooted is a good thing and that's the way Capricorn and often the partners you choose like to live your lives, but sometimes everyone needs a little bit of imagination, vision and the ability to stick your head in the clouds. So don't be afraid to do something a little outrageous or spontaneous because that could be the breath of fresh air the relationship needs.

Money and Finance

This month you've in quite a spendthrift mood, you may treat yourself. If you have a January birthday and if you've able to afford it, you may buy yourself a luxury item. Capricorn is normally quite thrifty and frugal but you're more likely to splash the cash and this month you will want to treat friends and family to a rather bigger than normal birthday celebration, so a lot of money gets spent on food, entertaining and items that will increase both your own pleasure and that of your guests.

You may also be more inclined to buy fine wine and redecorating your home is also something on which you might want to spend some money.

Living and Loving to the Full

This month to enhance love magic you and your partner need to be more open-minded and need to consider the ways in which you have become too rigid in your thinking. It's time to bounce ideas about with each other fearlessly, to encourage each other to express ideas without fear of criticism or castigation and simply experience the spark of truth.

It's time for you both to stop self-censoring, if you feel that you're walking on eggshells with each other, now it's time to ask why, and to reassess where the fun has been lost in the relationship? Is it because you are both too controlled and careful about what you say? It's time to be a little bite the bullet and to call it as you both see it and to be able to say what's on each other's mind.

Planetary Cautions

This month it's really important for you to avoid making promises you can't keep, it's often better for you to clear the deck, get everything ticked off your to-do list and put a strong focus on completing what you have started, rather than beginning any new projects.

So the key for you this month is detoxifying and simplify your life, both in an emotional way and in terms of work. So you don't want to be adding any more to your current itinerary. You must recognize a need for everything to be trimmed down so that you've ready to face the year and with a clean slate. You don't want to muddy the water as the key is keep things simple, that's why new relationships are better kept at arm's length and you shouldn't rush into any new financial arrangements either.

It's also an important time for some reflection and some down time, so you don't want to start the year too overstretched.

Moon Magic

The new moon phase extends from the 21th of January to the 5th of February, this waxing phase is the perfect fortnight for new initiatives, setting plans, establishing goals, starting anything prospective and being proactive. This is the action phase, details below:

Mercury goes direct on 19th in Capricorn indicating that the communications sphere, negotiations, discussions in marriage, relationship communication, debating and presenting your ideas is able to go ahead with aplomb.

Sun Sextile Jupiter at the new moon favors money matters, getting loans, rearranging debt and improving your financial position. It's favorable for all business involving audit, accounting and tax. It's also perfect for discussions about financial planning in marriage.

Venus Conjunct Saturn indicates this is not a good time for new career directions, new business ventures and changes in life goals. Not a perfect time for major new initiatives in changing life direction. PR, public events and public speaking or job interviews are not favored.

This is not the best waxing phase for dating and new romance. You should also avoid launching creative projects. Sports and competitive activities are not successful. It's important to be cautious in business involving leisure, entertainment and the arts.

A good period for personal goals, recuperating and improving health through physical activity or therapy. This favors doing physical work or exercise. An excellent time to express yourself with clarity and honesty and communicate in a positive way with people, including in relationships. Careers in modeling and acting are successful.

Mars goes direct in Gemini on the 13th bringing about momentum for activities involving exercise, diet and fitness. This also helps you in getting organized, improving your systems at work becoming more efficient. This helps you achieve goals within your work with more energy. Teamwork is not advisable. Manufacturing, carpentry and service orientated careers get a boost. Recruitment and training staff is successful.

Essence and Energies – "I have a talent, a wonderful thing!"

The essence this month is creativity, leadership and fun!

This month I want you to revitalize your energy by doing things that make you feel youthful, inspired and also bring you in contact with opportunities where you can shine. This is not a time to hide your light under a bushel, this is a time to seek opportunities to lead or showcase your talents. Whether you are naturally effervescent and outgoing, or whether you are one of the shy and reserved Capricorn, this is a time when you should be doing things that express your unique potentials.

It's important for you to engage in hobbies or activities where you can make your mark on the world, where you can create something or have total control of a process from start to finish, and which you feel that is a unique expression of yourself.

This month is also a great opportunity for you to have a good time and there's no reason you shouldn't as long as you are making some effort to meet your daily obligations. You should be free-spirited and spontaneous, if there's something that has ignited your interest, go for it! It's an excellent time to do things on the spur of the moment, which includes spontaneous outings, going to events on the spur of the moment or alternatively accepting social invites where there's a chance of romance.

This is your time to look for a stage on which you can perform, so express yourself don't hold back and enjoy this month.

Affirmation: "I deserve fun and excitement in my life and it's my duty to follow my star."

Love and Romance

This is an excellent month for love and relationships to blossom, it's a time when the romantic within Capricorn is stimulated. Now Capricorn is a big ol' softie inside and you've really drawn to extremely romantic, compassionate, sensible and protective types, So a new relationship is often very caring in nature and you'll be a lot more open with a new person, you may begin to share your deepest feelings and secrets far more early than you normally would, and a new relationship can become quite spiritually close and tender quickly.

This is an excellent time for long distance relationships or relationships that begin online where you guys don't meet, but you exchange lots of very loving or sentimental messages. Some Capricorn may be inspired to write music or poetry for a new love interest. Certainly this month is a month where your romantic idealist is stimulated and you find love a wonderful way to escape and feed your imagination.

This month it's important for you to ask yourself why you are feeling stuck or restricted in your romantic or love life, you need to look at the forces within yourself that draw you into these situations, or you need to understand whether you are perceiving the situations correctly. Once you've done that, it's time to smash through those barriers and get rid of a sense of hopelessness, and rather look forward with optimism knowing that the power is in your hands to change the trajectory of your relationship.

So it's time for stopping 'fearing the worst and hoping for the best' and making a conscious effort to strive to live your best life with your partner or with your future perfect partner, it all begins with your attitude.

Career and Aspiration

This is a very busy month in terms of your job, it's also very hands-on. It's an important time to pay attention to customer service and deadlines, it's also very important in terms of motivating teams and other staff members, and providing little bit of leadership to make sure everyone pulls their weight and is encouraged to meet deadlines.

This is a time when you may get promoted to a managerial or leadership role, so it's quite good for promotion in terms of your daily job, but that doesn't necessarily mean a career move into a different direction totally.

This is a fantastic time for any Capricorn who are setting up a business, as you have a lot of gusto and motivation, and you're great at dealing with detail, rolling your sleeves up and getting stuck in with setting all the cogs and wheels in motion to begin a new business.

So the keywords this month are: action; attending to details; getting organized and paying attention to customer and client needs.

Adventure and Motivation

This month you've very tuned in and sensitive to what is beautiful aesthetically, you have excellent taste and you are more inspired and captivated by the arts, so this is a wonderful time for you to go to theatres, visit art galleries, go to the movies or read books etc. because you find it quite emotionally uplifting to get involved in the arts.

Capricorn like to live vicariously through other people this month, and so even if you don't have a romance on the go, you can find the creative art forms a wonderful way to connect emotionally with the whole romantic and love sphere. So whatever your relationship status, you can find a lot of satisfaction emotionally through the arts or literature particularly romantic literature.

This is a month where it's great to mingle with different sorts of people and put yourself in circumstances that you wouldn't normally be in. The key right now is firing up your imagination thus Capricorn should get more in touch with your creative side, and often hanging out with artistic and more bohemian people is a fantastic way for you to see possibilities that you might not see within your regular cliques and walks of life.

So it's important to be socially adventurous and it's also important to be more versatile in terms of the activities you choose to engage in in your free time, and remember free time is everything right now, all work and no play makes Jack a dull boy.

Marriage and Family

This is a time of hard work and serious discussions in marriage, you and a partner need to be able to show each other commitment and to reinforce trust and cooperation.

It's very important in marriages to be pragmatic and realistic, but that doesn't mean that you and your partner shouldn't share some fun and some tender moments, but it's a case of working hard as well as playing hard.

In love, you and your partner need to be serious about tackling difficulties, you need to pull together and both show strength and emotional restraint in dealing with family and relationship problems. On the other hand you also need to make time for fun date nights and recapturing romance, so all work and no play makes you dull, but it's not time to overlook serious issues or be ostriches either.

The key in love relationships this month is not falling under the misapprehension that you are imprisoned by external forces that are ultimately out of your control. Too often in life we are fatalistic, we accept things as they are, in many cases with good grace, but sometimes it's important to say enough is enough, I am going to take control and I am going to write the script.

So whatever has gone on in your relationship life before, and whether you are in a relationship or looking for a relationship, this is your opportunity to change your mindset or your perspective, and therefore start writing a different script that can either take your marriage in a much better direction, or revolutionize the way you go into new relationships.

This is time to feel like you are master of your own destiny, you need to be aware of the tricks that fate plays. You have free will and you can remove any restrictions or impediments, be they physical or psychological with determination, and then you can reduce the influence that fate has over you.

Money and Finance

This is a month where you need to carefully plan your expenditure, but you need to ensure that there's sufficient cash flow to account for various shocks and surprises. It's not a good month for investing in the stock market or doing anything speculative, even if you are rather conservative there will still be surprises, so you don't want to increase risk and volatility by doing things that you don't have a lot of experience in or knowledge about.

It's a good month for planning, and also great for gathering information and making sure you understands what's going on in the wider economy, but you need to stay ever ready for big news and major changes that can affect you financially.

Living and Loving to the Full

This is a good time for surprises and may be great for you to surprise your partner with flowers, chocolates and a trip to the theatre, if money allows. On the other hand, it can also be a lot of fun to attend sporting events, even if it's only the children playing a ball game, because often the fun and excitement of a high school college match helps you and a partner recapture a little bit of their youthful spirit, and supporting the children can bring couples together.

This is also a great time for you guys to do novel things with your children, be they older or younger or whether you have a blended family. It's great to spend time with kids and in a relaxed informal setting where you can all let your hair down and enjoy yourselves. So get out with the whole family, as it's also a great way to relax.

Planetary Cautions

This may not be the greatest time for you to be working with other people, sometimes other people are very erratic and unreliable, especially when you have to co-ordinate over management or possibly creative issues.

When Capricorn is working on a problem or an idea, you need to have freedom, you don't want to have anyone standing in your way, and that's why activities that involve you following your own initiative or working to your own timetable are much more suitable. Teamwork can be extremely frustrating for you and also inhibiting, and should be avoided.

You really have a sweet tooth right now and therefore it's easy to pile on the calories, so one of your challenges this month is to avoid the high carb, sugary food and opt for more fish, legumes and organic meat.

Another potential problem this month is not knowing when enough is enough, you need to understand where to draw a line. So boundaries are important, this pertains more to your work life and your relationships with colleagues and clients rather than personal relationships, but it's important not to over deliver, otherwise you can leave yourself stretched and quite exhausted by trying to put that cherry on top when it could be unnecessary or unappreciated.

Moon Magic

The new moon phase extends from the 20th of February to the 7th of March, this waxing phase is the perfect fortnight for new initiatives, setting plans, establishing goals, starting anything prospective and being proactive. This is the action phase, details below:

The waxing phase is excellent for new business contracts, financial organization and purchasing assets. It's a great waxing phase for reaching targets, developing investment strategies and money management. Increases in income or getting a pay rise or opening a new income stream is favored.

Excellent for home improvements. Property and real estate matters are favored. A good time for large family events, entertaining and celebrations. Renovations and adaptation of the home is favored. Great for business involving catering, hospitality and the environment. Good for organizing a home office or doing more work or study from home. Excellent for management decisions in businesses that involve the environment, hospitality or care industry.

This is a good phase for new diets and beginning health initiatives. An excellent time to join a gym and have a better attitude to health and fitness. Good for on the job training, learning new skills and recruiting staff. A time to improve relationships with colleagues or staff. Educational and medical careers are favored. Dealing with animals is favored.

Essence and Energies – "Dreams are for those who sleep "

This month the energy is very much about new ideas, enthusiasm and the mental spark.

Right now it's excellent to capture the planetary momentum and get started on a new project or an idea, especially one that you can share with others. This is an excellent time, not only for new projects and ventures, but also for new journeys. It's important for you to feel excited and any activity that enlivens you and gives you a sense of adventure is certainly something that you need to embrace.

Curiosity is an important element of the energies this month, they saying that necessity is the mother of all invention, but I say curiosity is the mother of all enterprise, because often once something has sparked your interest and you begin to follow it like a dog with a sent, you suddenly uncover exciting things that can be lead to new directions. So this month I want you to follow that scent, if there's something that interests you, or excites you, go with it see where it leads.

The one challenge is being able to keep up with yourself, sometimes your ideas race ahead faster than the practical plans, so you don't want to jump in at the deep end, however things look very promising so keep a steady pace.

Affirmation: "Variety and new ideas are the spice of life and I am happy to embrace these."

Love and Romance

Capricorn have to watch out for the mirage effect in love, all that glitters is not gold; you can idealistic about your friendships and may overstate their romantic potential in your mind. Sudden sexual liaisons with friends are possible – Capricorn are easily turned on, and you may make a move on a long-term friend; this often does not work out, but it could well suit you guys both temporarily.

This can be a tricky time for new relationships in which you guys have very different outlooks politically, religiously and regarding world view – while you both may have been able to ignore these gaps in understanding so far, now you are coming up against issues which tend to be informed by belief.

This tends to be quite an emotional period, you may wear your heart on your sleeve, you may come across as a little bit needy. On a positive note, you may be more likely to engage with others in a positive and productive way forming interesting new relationships with potential problems.

It's important to weigh up your options and use good judgement, this can be a time of moral dilemmas in relationships and therefore you must take time over any decisions and be using wise cool headed logic. Don't capitulate to a bossy or dramatic partner.

Career and Aspiration

It's a busy month filled with the unexpected, nothing can be assumed and so the diary entries must be made in pencil, so everything can be rubbed out and rewritten.

Your daily routine may be anything but routine as you get pulled hither and thither by chance events. It's a hectic time when you have to just be flexible and make the most of it, but it's not humdrum. It is one of those time where it is not about what you know but who you know and so if you are out of the loop it can take great effort to work your way to the inside, but you can do it as long as you commit to that goal.

It is vital for you to address your work habits and routines, especially where these are already having or may have an impact on your long term health. Slower recovery from things like colds and flus can be an indication that you're run down, stressed or that bad habits are having a long term effect and this is an ideal time to tackle these.

They say 'seek and you will find' and this month it's vital for you to seek information, and by seeking that information, you will not only find solutions you will find wisdom.

You can be slightly idealistic and you are more likely to think about the future, you can be quite unrestrained in the way you plan and envisage things and this is excellent because you don't want to be boxed in in your thinking.

While some people can stand in your way, it's important to identify those whom you can align with, who will not overwhelm you or stifle your direction, but who instead will support you, encourage your ideas and want to unite with you in fulfilling them.

Adventure and Motivation

This is a time of new ideas on a spiritual level and you may be drawn to religion or awareness raising teachings which help you to make sense of life. Often day to day activities satisfy less and you crave a deeper meaning to join the dots: that may be found via travel, especially cultural trips or by sailing or being close to the ocean. Capricorn crave truth and yet you desires a different kind of truth, something more universal perhaps involving karma or fate. Capricorn are more in touch with emotions and your intuition is enhanced, helping you to make decisions fast, unlike your usual cautious and pragmatic self. You may quite surprise yourself in terms of the way you become subjective and very flexible in terms of embracing the bizarre and unusual.

There is a strong desire within you to pay back favors, you have a peculiar sense of divine justice and are keen to make ethical and fair decisions as you feel like you've being judged and karma will not look kindly on you should you get it wrong. In 2023, you err on the side of caution and you often give more than you need to in any situation as you want to be sure your slate is clean.

Marriage and Family

The month may begin with arguments and tempers and you guys may find yourselves at odds especially about money, but also in connection with judgement. Your partner may agree with you on the facts, but you may have a very different moral or ethical conclusion about how to handle those facts. You may even feel dismayed or disappointed in your partner's attitude, but you can't convince them of your point of view as we are talking here about personality differences, not just temporary differences of opinion. It can be a new learning phase in relationships, as you guys face issues you never have faced before and in the process learn things about each other you never knew.

One of you will have to compromise, but be pragmatic and don't take it as an ego defeat, it's just life.

Later in the month is generally calm in love, although there are a still a few tensions that lurk beneath the surface. You may feel a sense of detachment, as if your partner is not present enough or connected enough. However, there is nothing you can put your finger on, and so it is very hard for you to communicate your feelings. You tend to need more support and reassurance, but it's hard to get that and so you may just be a little difficult or uncooperative to almost jolt your partner and make them take notice.

Money and Finance

In some cases, you're painfully aware of your need for change and yet you also know that you will have to get radical or uncomfortable to achieve this. This year the manner in which things get done is in short sharp bursts, rather than in a systematic step by step fashion. The month in particular may not flow, it either surges or stalls and sometimes the baby gets thrown out with the bath water as you can get frustrated. It's all very creative however and sudden insights can render previous ideas null and void, or can boost ideas to you help them take off.

Living and Loving to the Full

You may want to take a few small risks in love this March – now what you regards as 'risk' really depends on the current state of romantic life, but a risk could be anything from trying a new way to meet a partner, breaking a rule you have set for yourself, i.e. no workplace romances, asking someone you hardly knows out, etc. If you've already in a relationship, a risk may mean suggesting a new sexual toy or activity. It could even mean talking about a sexual problem you guys have not had the ability to talk about before. If you takes the bull by the horns, you may surprise yourself. Not taking risks means getting into ruts, which can be both boring and self-defeating – break the mold this month and do something romantically or sexually that you would not usually do.

Planetary Cautions

This may not be a good time for financial negotiations as there are too many unknowns and too much ambivalence among the parties.

This is not a great time for legal and financial dealings or analysis. It's good for you to stay flexible and keep an open mind.

Emotions can cloud judgment especially if you are already in an upset frame of mind, so you shouldn't take important decisions when emotional.

You must not believe everything you hear, be skeptical and don't get led up the garden path.

The transits this month can lead to overreactions and exaggerated emotional states. You are likely to jump the gun and to behave hastily and subjectively. This magnifies your emotional responses and you go with your heart and that may lead you to take more risks, be more judgmental or create conflict with others.

Food allergies are exacerbated this month and you again need to be cautious about diet.

Food allergies are exacerbated by this transit and you are also less cautious about what you eat meaning you may gain weight or indulge in alcohol.

Moon Magic

The new moon phase extends from the 21st of March to the 6th of April, this waxing phase is the perfect fortnight for new initiatives, setting plans, establishing goals, starting anything prospective and being proactive. This is the action phase, details below:

The waxing phase is not good for new artistic ventures and self-expression. Dating and social activities organized to meet potential partners are not successful. Not favorable for competitive sports and or coaching teams. New business involving children is not advisable. Creativity and invention is more difficult. Not great for launching artistic or entertainment projects to the public. Not favorable for business involving leisure and fun.

An excellent waxing period for family discussions or organizing important family events. Suitable for planning home improvements or house hunting. New business involving hospitality, care and real estate are favored. Good for organizing pensions and long term savings. Suitable for study, research and dealing with personal matters. A good time to be more private and to consolidate and prepare. Good for clear-outs and improving the home in connection with working from home. Great for research and fiction writing or in depth study. Green initiatives and environmental issues are important. Good for consolidation and making savings. Great for dealing with private matters.

New roles at work or recruitment of staff is not favored, nor is traveling to attend a course. This is not a successful time for new diets, innovative health initiatives and anything strict or restrictive in terms of diet. Not a good time to join a gym or begin a new fitness regime. Training staff is not successful. Not a favorable time to open a business connected to animals, manufacturing or medicine.

The waxing phase isn't ideal for PR, public events and public speaking. Business leadership, job interviews and new management strategies are not favored. Compliance and understanding the protocols or respecting authority is important. Not a great time for brand new career or business management decisions.

***Essence and Energies – "Are you reelin' in the years?
Stowin' away the time?"***

The energy this month is all about nostalgia, connecting with our roots and enjoying reminiscing. It's always important to show gratitude and to return to our roots as a way of replenishing ourselves in an earthy and a spiritual way.

It's always important to remember happy times, especially when you do it with other family members as it reinforces that important bond we have with our nearest and dearest.

Memories are aspects of the past, which reflect the parts of our journey and also perhaps elements of ourselves that have vanished. It may be that remembering these times is a pathway to happiness and feeling contented to something. So while I don't advocate living in the past, it's important to understand how the past brought us to where we are today and the important relationships we formed along the way.

Part of the activities this month, when exploring your essence and connecting with your roots may be returning to a familiar place. This could be your hometown, an old friend's home, a school, visiting older relatives going to any place that holds a lot of meaning for you. You should seek to reconnect with people from your past, reviving old memories that remind you of a time when life was simpler and in this way you can escape the present to gain a perspective.

Affirmation: "I appreciate all the experiences in my life as part of my unique and precious journey."

Love and Romance

In general this is a quite an interesting month for romance, in ongoing romantic relationships communication is improving and there should be a lot of fun and compatibility. New relationships formed right now are quite free flowing and have an almost seamless start, however what you do have to worry about is superficiality in relationships as often someone is putting their best foot forward, but there may be something more to be discovered. The next few months will cast a new light on the relationship, so while you should have fun and enjoy new relationships and dating, you shouldn't assume that you know everything about a new partner.

You are feeling very sociable this month and you have a need to express your romantic and passion nature, which is something Capricorn possess in abundance even if you don't wear it on your sleeve. Your added sexual energy, could encourage you to make a move on a potential person you fancy or to spontaneously accept invites to dating events or parties.

Your interactions with people will be more intense and exciting, and you may need to exert some control over your enthusiasms, in office or work situations. This is definitely a time when you are more likely to feel that spark of attraction and a quickening of the pulse when you see a hot guy.

This isn't the best time for starting a long distance relationship or one based in meetings remotely. Chemistry is very important and so physical attraction in real life is the only good barometer of relationship potential.

Career and Aspiration

This month it's important for you to work on customer relations and service. It's a great time to improve your reputation by adding value to your services with bonuses and extras.

Cooperation with colleagues is important, but should remain professional, this is not a good time to mix business with pleasure.

You should fully commit to ongoing assignments and make sure that you complete these in time as deadlines count. It's important for you to be loyal to your trusted colleagues, supplies or regular clients and to prioritize them. It's a time to consolidate good relationships at work or in your supply chain through good communication. A strong sense of duty is the way to impress, but you should still maintain bounds without going over the top to please clients.

In April tried and tested routines tend to deliver results, whereas newfangled or overcomplicated approaches can lead to waste. So old fashioned communication and customer service win the day.

Adventure and Motivation

This is an excellent time for you to initiate changes that will have a long term effect on your lifestyle or psychological health. You can introduce new positive habits or find information that will open up exciting new avenues of thought that enable you to break free of repressive mindsets and negative cycle of behavior.

You may have experiences, personal or through your employment, that leave an indelible impression on you and serve as a catalyst for taking steps, even quite radical measures to transform what is worn out and defunct in your life. It's a time of potential renewal and greater freedom, which stems from AHA moments when the truth about certain situations dawns.

By paying attention to the signals from the universe and using these as a catalyst for internal review and adjustment, you can grow exceptionally stronger by planting the right seeds now.

Affirmations which encourage you to recognize your own power in any situation are very helpful and yield exciting results that can bring an internal adventure into your life.

Marriage and Family

This is a time of pressing concerns in relationships and the most important thing is getting priorities straight. There are often competing needs and concerns and you can't take them on at the same time, you and your partner, or you alone if your partner is not able or willing, must make a judgement call on where to apply energy and focus and then things should be tackled systematically. This is not a period where a scattered or halfhearted effort can cut through the problems.

Difficult decisions must be made, but things usually get a lot easier once they are and clarity is created.

The changes or plans made now as a result of pressure, are always in your best interest, although it may not seem so at the time. The more you acknowledge challenges, or obstacles and begin to sort through them with determination, the most your own inner peace and security, increases and this draws strength into the relationship.

Anything that distracts from key priorities must be sidelined, as you and your partner rid yourselves of inessential elements in your personal life.

You're more emotionally sensitive during April and even little things your partner does can frustrate you more than usual. You're likely to experience more moodiness or to be more reactionary in relationships, and you should watch out for letting things get out of control. Remember to take a deep breath and count to ten. You need space and you don't always enjoy long conversations or very sterile and static situations, whereas you enjoy doing physically exerting things with your partner. So couples that play together, thrive together.

Sometimes in love you feel the need to defend yourself but may be unsure of why you're reacting so vehemently, you can get hot under the collar. Often explosive events now may be in response to anger that's been building from the past, or something that happens now may remind you of a past dispute, but you can preempt that by acknowledging anger and forgiving and releasing that bad energy.

If you and your partner have had a stressful phase in your relationship, spending time mulling over the great times you have spent together, and perhaps reliving them, can bring you great comfort.

Money and Finance

This is a month of redefining or getting more clarity in financial arrangements. Reading fine print or getting more idea about your rights and obligations in any contract is important.

You may consolidate or rearrange debt or remortgage. This is a time to be more creative about your financial affairs are arranged.

In business partnerships, differences of opinion between you and others can cause temporary breakdown and the issue of trust may arise in certain relationships. It's time for you to start extracting yourself from any financial contact or arrangement where trust and transparency has broken down.

Living and Loving to the Full

This can definitely be an exciting time in relationships, although if not handled correctly it can be quite contentious. Capricorn tends to be quite amorous and you're eager to re-engage sexually as your sensual side comes to the fore. Now Capricorn can be a big old teddy bear, but you certainly enjoy getting the creative juices flowing in the bedroom too, so this is an excellent time to spice up your sex life.

It can be a good idea to go on date night involving vigorous activity like sports or dancing, or go to see a movie that really gets the adrenaline pumping, because you have quite a high need for excitement and stimulation and so cozy candle lit dinners really won't do it. It's a time to find something to get excited about as a couple and allow that to bring you together and reignite the spark.

This month it's important to bury the hatchet, let bygones be bygones and so that you can move forward.

Remember that forgiving others doesn't free them, or let them off the hook, it frees you. So release yourself and forgive and let go as it's important to achieve closure this month.

It's important to arrest any aggressive or conflict areas of life, stop them in their tracks and move towards diplomacy. Nothing can be gained now through bad feeling and arguing, so try to encourage resolution.

Look beyond what's happened in the past to find a way through any current crisis or challenge that you are facing now, it's time to break the spell or shackles of past patterns.

Planetary Cautions

This month Mercury is in Taurus and it goes retrograde on the 21st, so while first three weeks of the month are excellent for problem-solving, making management decisions and organizing creative projects, you must be aware that after the 21st there can be some problems and delays and therefore it's best to get things moving right at the front part of the month, and use the latter part of the month for analysis, fine-tuning and getting more organized.

While the first part of the month can be quite exciting for internet dating, after Mercury retrograde, there can be a lot of misunderstandings in new relationships so you have to proceed cautiously. You should be wary of inappropriate jokes and you just need to think twice before you speak, so while you shouldn't walk on eggshells, it's important to be diplomatic.

Moon Magic

The new moon phase extends from the 20th of April to the 5th of May this waxing phase is the perfect fortnight for new initiatives, setting plans, establishing goals, starting anything prospective and being proactive. This is the action phase, details below:

The waxing phase is still good for planning family events, house hunting and real estate deals. This period is suitable for work from home initiatives and also doing private research. Home improvements and home decorating are successful. You may invite people to say. An excellent time for restaurant business.

Favorable for financial reorganization. Money matters connected to loans, taxes and debt can be tackled. A time to do research on financial matters and get clarity. Sex counseling or better communication about sex is important. Investigation and discovery of difficult information is valuable. Good for getting tips and donations. Excellent waxing phase for careers involving tax, insurance and accounting matters.

Mercury goes retrograde in Taurus on the 21st meaning the start of a more confusing time for dating, social activities and it's tricky meeting new potential partners. It's less favorable for creativity and artistic work in career or as a hobby and precision must be favored over speed or progress. Sports and leisure activities can have unexpected outcomes. Business aimed at young people, entertainment or leisure need a rethink.

MAY

Essence and Energies – "Let the sun shine in."

This is an excellent month of abundance and radiance. The essence is to enhance your strength and vitality by soaking up the sun, being outdoors and doing life-affirming activities. You should indulge yourself by doing activities that make you feel alive and happy, don't delay, grab you piece of the happiness pie today. This is not a time to be restrained or self-denying.

By actively seeking your own personal fulfillment, you recharge your batteries and can provide others with inspiration and joy as well. People will be drawn to your confidence and charm as you are exuding a warm and beautiful energy.

This month you should strive to share your creativity as well as achievements with other people. Radiate love and affection towards those you care about the most.

This is a month to reflect on your relationships with other people, you may be the beacon of light that serves as an inspiration for someone else. You may be compelled to help lead and support others using your experience, positivity and intuitive abilities.

Think with your heart, instead of your mind. Lead others with rationality and common sense, but don't discount the power of showing strength and following the light.

Affirmation: "I embrace the best of life, I seek to enjoy and reward myself and then I spread light to others."

Love and Romance

This is an excellent time for brand new activities in your life and for being a little bit out there, so if there's been anything which you've been wanting to do for a while, you should grab the opportunity, it doesn't necessarily have to involve romance, but often doing things that are close to your heart and following your inspiration leads to great romantic opportunities.

This is definitely a time when you should embrace novelty and the unorthodox in love, you shouldn't worry about ticking boxes or looking for a certain type, you should rather throw yourself into the social scene and whatever will be will be. It's a great time for you to try and interact with people that you don't normally associate with, so joining new clubs and organizations that represent hobbies that you haven't tried before is an outstanding way to be exposed to different personalities and to get away from your usual cliques, because that is the key to love.

In existing love relationships tolerance is very important and the more open-minded you is, and willing to embrace the quirks of your partner, the better.

In new relationships, stay flexible and don't count on any particular outcome, as any surprises now could be an opportunity to move in a better direction.

You may pursue a new partnership with a guy who's very different from you, but it's best to wait until the end of this month to see if it's really viable.

Career and Aspiration

This is an excellent time for creative activities or for launching any entertainment or creative event, it is also suitable for those Capricorn involved in the leisure industry. In terms of your work it's always important to use fresh new ideas, so this is an excellent time to introduce anything novel in either the way you do your work, promote your business or deal with your customers.

You should also try and be more creative in the way you update your profile on all social media, so you may want to put fresh pictures, memes, images or information on all your social media profiles to stimulate interest in these sites.

There are often opportunities to unite with others and create something together or complement each other. It's important to cooperate and not to compete. Often competing means you focus on undermining others rather than seeing synergies and ways in which cooperation helps you all to succeed

The thoroughness of your planning, along with a versatile approach and the use of your foresight will help guarantee the success of any project now, especially those involving other people, law, negotiation and justice.

Adventure and Motivation

What's important for Capricorn this month is getting in touch with what really inspires and excites you, it's time for you to think of all of those things you do simply because it's necessary or out of obligation, and to think about what you do that truly adds value to your life. It's time to inject excitement into your life again, to not be tired to old routines or convention.

It's a wonderful opportunity this month for you to strike out in an entirely new direction, and this can help you to meet new friends and experience different ideas. May can be an excellent time for you to get involved in activism or politics, it's also great time to get involved in something that has a larger role beyond yourself like a humanitarian or charitable project.

Marriage and Family

During this time Capricorn tend to be more materially minded and you will definitely want to talk to your partner about how to save money, invest and maybe even prepping. You are quite aware of events in the economy and you're concerned about the future more so than usual so you want to take a 'be prepared' attitude.

In marriage, you're eager to have conversations about far-reaching issues, so rather than chatting about day-to-day stuff with your partner, you may want to talk about long-term future plans for where to live, and pensions and sometimes these conversations can open up a few cans of worms. So a lot of what you want to talk about this month with your partner can lead into to avenue of conversation that both of you may find quite surprising, and this can reveal many differences in opinion or values that you didn't know were there before. However, it's still important to have these conversations right now because they can be quite revealing and even helpful for the relationship in the longer term.

Money and Finance

This month significant events can lead to changes in thinking about money or give you exciting new ideas. Often following a new idea right now could be quite disruptive and it may cause a break in the flow of your career, so it's likely that you will spend a lot of time this month on something outside of your normal concern. If you've got a regular job, you might spend a lot more time on a hobby on the side which you hope will lead to another form of employment later on.

This month is a time when in general you have to put a lot more thought into money matters that are not connected to your regular employment, so it might be the case that you have to help other people or family members with their money problems, or even spend more time helping your partner sort out her finances.

Living and Loving to the Full

This is an excellent month for spontaneity and it's really good for Capricorn and your partner to get amongst your friends or go to large gatherings and group experiences like concerts or even trade fairs.

It may be quite rewarding for Capricorn and your partner to work on a project together, maybe organizing a group event, a party or working within your networks. Often doing social activities together that are also linked to work and supporting each other in that way can reignite your love magic.

It's an important month to show each other that you care by being each other's cheerleaders, supporters and showing a lot of camaraderie and support for each other's projects, hopes and dreams.

Planetary Cautions

The Mercury retrograde period affects your 5th house and the sphere of romance is highlighted, although caution is needed as there can be misunderstandings.

You need to go with your head in love during this period, to set emotion and sentimentality aside and to be objective. If you are rather maudlin or heart on sleeve, then you've not necessarily going to make good decisions in this frame of mind.

You can suddenly get cold feet in new relationships and so relationships can be stop start. In relationships in general, you may suddenly need a bit more space or you could demand an injection of excitement with new social activities.

To keep you happy in bed your partner needs to be spontaneous and creative, using music and aesthetically appealing clothing. You need compliments and date nights, weekends away are essential, you both need a break from work.

Moon Magic

The new moon phase extends from the 19th of May to the 3rd of June this waxing phase is the perfect fortnight for new initiatives, setting plans, establishing goals, starting anything prospective and being proactive. This is the action phase, details below:

The waxing phase is great for marriage, engagement and positive events in marriage. It's good for initiating discussion and healing in love relationships. Team work, new business partnerships, consulting and legal matters are favored. A good waxing phase for getting good advice from experts.

An excellent waxing phase for arranging finances, investing or purchasing new equipment or assets for your business. Good for creating more affection and security in a relationship.

A good period for investing, budgeting and buying assets for your business. Great for increased cash flow and getting new clients.

Good for greater respect and trust in relationships.

Great period for trying new things, meeting new people or going to new places. Excellent period for new health initiatives. Sports and competitive activities are favored. Ideal for personal goals and being assertive.

Caution is needed in planning religious events for family occasions. Promotional and publishing activities may not be successful.

The waxing phase is excellent for foreign travel or long journeys. Publishing and educational or academic goals are favored.

A good waxing phase for learning new skills and refining and perfecting your projects or written work. Client feedback is important. Better communication with colleagues and the people you serves is important. You may need a second opinion on medical matters. A good time for medical research to investigate better health solutions. Great for new diets and fitness regimes.

**_Essence and Energies – "I can't offer you proof
But you're gonna face a moment of truth."_**

This month is rich in symbolism and meaning. It's important to be alert to symbols and messages from the universe.

It's vital to understand the ebbs and flows of life and to understand contrast. Nothing in life can be fully appreciated without contrast, light and dark, good and bad, up and down.

Respect these natural flows, reflect on what you cannot control and release that need for control. Capricorn often like to be like Atlas taking the weight of the world on your shoulders, but it's not all for you to do, learn to let go and trust in the universe or the benevolence of mother nature.

Appreciate the good moments in your life, and enjoy them to the fullest, but what goes up must always come down, but same is true in reverse - so wherever you are struggling in life, have faith that there will be a turnaround.

Understanding these cycles is vital in being able to release a lot of the weight of responsibility you feel and this reduces stress.

There are more forces outside of your control right now, some may call it luck, randomness or fate, but either way, know when not to fight it. Be positive, think optimistically and focus on awareness, personal growth and not always just solutions as you pass through these inevitable cycles.

Affirmation: "I have faith and trust and I know when these are more important than control."

Love and Romance

This month you need a philosophical approach in love to create a balance between your increasingly impulsive heart and your more pragmatic

Capricorn head. You need emotional maturity, and to exercise some self-control, but you don't want to be too restrained as you cannot deny your need for adventure through relationships.

Emotional tensions run high, you've not your usual calm and collected Capricorn self, however this month is just what you need to open doors for yourself romantically and to connect with women/men in a more deep and satisfying way.

You should use both logic and intuition in your approach to love, although you've passionate and excitable you must approach romance with practicality, but also with wisdom, compassion and understanding.

There's some amazing stuff happening in romance and you should let your hair down, but at the same time you don't want to destroy new romantic opportunities by jumping the gun.

Career and Aspiration

Your natural sense of determination is enhanced this month and you've got an enormous appetite to get things done.

You're inspired to initiate projects that are long term, intimidating or quite intense and you will aim to improve or reform your attitudes to work, to money or to the people that you work with. You're more aware of power and control issues and possibly office politics, and thus you're likely to be more strategic and careful about how you go about things.

You have far less interest in pursuing goals that are superficial or trivial. Often your desire and intensity will be hard to contain and thus you're easily set off by criticism, and you can get quite angry when people stand in your way. You will not give up however, when thwarted you simply recalibrate and come back in a different way.

You've very skilled in managing money, both your own and that of others, and you've got the courage to face facts and truths which others are avoiding, which means that you're more likely to make headway while others are in denial.

An excellent month for scientific development, creating apps or crypto currency development. IT and graphic design projects are successful.

Adventure and Motivation

You're fascinated by what's obscure or under the radar, and you're looking to investigate and explore the deeper aspects of your work or your personal life.

You may delve in politics or news stories looking for the inside track. You may analysis financial data looking for trends or you could look to psychology to uncover the secrets of your own or your partner's personality. Whatever it is, you want to understand things at a far more esoteric level and thus get to a breakthrough moment. Your main sense of adventure this month comes through deep analysis and thoughtfulness about the real workings of things.

In some cases you look to illicit love affairs or flings for a chance to escape and get a taste of the exotic. Often your heightened desire level and need for danger or intrigue lead you into some strange places.

You have a good balance of enthusiasm, and restraint of ambition and caution, which enables you to capitalize on opportunities and evaluate opportunities with a clear head. This is a period of intense learning and you may find that a new aspect of your career or new subject grabs your attention, and it blossoms into something very important to you both financially or spiritually.

There are often significant opportunities right now which end up changing the course of your life, these could be in your personal or business life. It's important to focus on what you enjoy and follow your passion, but you should maintain a steady pace and be realistic. If you seek fulfillment through what you most enjoy and hone your talents and abilities, and if you have a high level of self-awareness, there's no end to what you can achieve during this Month.

Marriage and Family

This month what's important in marriage is comforting each other and being compassionate and understanding.

It's important not to let words get in the way, too much conversation can actually over complicate things. Couples who enjoy meditation or share a faith are stronger this month than relationships that rely heavily on logic and debate. This is a month for being together in a relaxed, mindful way without overthinking your relationship. Capricorn is very intense this month and you can get overwrought, so you must have a space of calm in your relationship.

It's important for you and your partner to be physically affectionate and emotionally responsive as it's easy for you to feel isolated or lonely and so you crave an emotionally engaging partner.

You're often quite stressed in terms of work and so you need a partner who can relax you and bring you down to earth again. If your partner is also really stressed, you may both need a good night out or break to get away from it all.

Your commitment to your partner may be tested now, and both of you may have to put in some effort or sacrifice in order to remain together, this is usually pretty easy for Capricorn as you are psychologically geared to patience and loyalty, however now you will really get to see what your partner is made of, making this quite a revealing time. Good times often mask true intentions but difficult or testing times bring about important revelations and the secrets of you and your partner's hearts are revealed.

Your marriage or relationship has the potential to become closer and more meaningful than before as the two of you learn to navigate the ups and downs together as a team. It is vital to acknowledge that whether the ebbs and flows are positive or negative, nothing is forever, for the wheel is always turning and there is always a new way forward.

Money and Finance

Your ability to turn things around financially is enhanced as you're capable of making tough calls and using your grit to bite the bullet while you purge unnecessary spending or costs. Decisions this month are difficult, but when you have a plan you execute.

You may plunge headfirst into projects that promise great rewards, even if they may be controversial or place you at odds with your partner or others.

While success is possible now, you're punching above your weight and you've got to be careful not to push too far too soon.

You can get stuck in detail and rabbit holes and you must be really careful not to lose perspective as that's a big problem right now.

Living and Loving to the Full

Sharing secrets is essential to relationships. This month enhancing love magic is all about the intimate arena, how much do you trust each other, how much do you really share with each other? Often relationships go downhill because there is nothing that you share with each other that's unique. It's important for lovers to be confidantes who will divulge secrets that they will tell no one else. It's important that a couple come together for private discussion, sharing intimate thoughts and being in a space that's special and safe.

Capricorn needs to cultivate an intimate environment where you and your partner reveal all and share things personal to you both as this special sharing of deep emotions, fears, joys and fantasies is extremely beneficial to the relationship.

Planetary Cautions

Legal matters must be approached with great caution. You should avoid direct confrontation with others.

This is a good time for study in an informal setting, you hate anything too regimented or restrictive this month.

This month you need maximum flexibility and freedom in your work and leisure life. You should resist activities that require you to work to a schedule as you're at your best when you can go with the flow and act on inspiration or follow leads that come up.

You are creatively supercharged, but this is an idea generating time, not a good time for actualization or formal designing.

Moon Magic

The new moon phase extends from the 18th of June to the 3rd of July this waxing phase is the perfect fortnight for new initiatives, setting plans, establishing goals, starting anything prospective and being proactive. This is the action phase, details below:

The waxing phase is great for brand new activities and fresh starts. Improving health and recuperation is favored. A good time for physical activities, getting fitter or improving physical health with physiotherapy, reiki, acupuncture or chiropractic therapy.

Things tend to be confusing in terms of business negotiations, mediation and legal matters, and you should avoid concrete decisions on loans or new insurance or tax schemes.

Not suitable for investment and assets purchases. Not a great time for budgeting and organizing your financial affairs. New side hustles or new ways of earning money may not pan out.

This is a good time for renewed focus on organization, good routines and health. Service and quality is vital. Time to address minutia and understand the important details. A good time for medical matters and dealing with animals. A better time for dietary changes, getting fit and improving health holistically.

Sporting event are successful. Pursuits in the outdoors and nature are ideal. Good for generous and community spirited activities. Good for academic recognition and community leadership. Good for publishing and promoting your work. Long distance journeys are favored. Good for contemplating long term goals.

Real estate and home improvements are successful. Great for large family events, entertaining and having family to stay. Good for home decorating. New business is hospitality is favored.

Essence and Energies – "Reap the whirlwind."

The essence this month is connecting with your Capricorn ability to be stern but also fair. It's important to judge situations for what they are and take the lead in providing an objective point of view and exposing what is the truth.

You may be thrust into situations where you're drawn into conflict, have to negotiate or have to decide who's side to take, and you are well positioned to judge the situation appropriately and not to allow emotion to get in the way.

This is also a time when you have to encourage others to leave their emotions and egos on the shelf, so that everyone can remain as objective as possible, because progress and finding solutions this month is all about being rational and shutting out distractions.

While one should always be compassionate, it's important this month not to let your sympathy get in the way of judgement. We can all have empathy with people, but we still have to know right from wrong and that's where you have to draw the line.

Affirmation: "I am strong when I seek truth a follow logos."

Love and Romance

This month represents a turning point in romantic relationship. Is it working? Is it forward or backward looking? Is there chemistry? Is something substantial happening or is it just going through the motions.

You must recognize where you've become stuck in emotional dynamics or patterns that are no longer really working. If you're already in a love relationship, for this relationship to continue successfully, you must tweak a few things and not allow it just to drift along, so it may be the time to broach more challenging subjects and jump the relationship to a new level.

It could be the time to discuss how you guys can both get more satisfaction from the relationship sexually or emotionally.

It's possible that you may decide to end a relationship that's not really going anywhere, or where you feel the person lacks depth, or if there's little true compatibility or passion for each other.

If a new relationship is holding you back or rubbing salt into old wounds, it's best to end it. A relationship that's eerily similar to a previous failed relationship also has to go.

Capricorn can be guilty of always thinking about the longer term and wanting to plan it out, when the key right now is living the moment, so enjoy the moment and appreciate what you are gaining in terms of personal growth, without worrying about final outcome.

Career and Aspiration

This month is characterized by tests of your will and your self-belief, however if you can find a way through this can be a significant time for you discovering or rediscovering your true passion and growing in confidence.

Even if forces beyond your control or fate itself blocks your attempts to advance, this is just a test of your will and you'll only get stronger in your efforts to defend your principles and to advocate for yourself.

Using your Capricorn perseverance, and not taking NO for an answer, is key to you triumphing. You must believe in yourself and your ideas, but you must not lose sight of other options in your desire to prove that you are right.

It is important for Capricorn to pursue what really matters to you, not out of ego satisfaction, but from the depth of your being, or else you may find any victory less than fulfilling.

Adventure and Motivation

In July, there are many opportunities for experiences that can help you in the realization of what is actually best for you, it's a time of coincidences and messages from the universe, and often you won't like these messages as you think you know what's best, but in reality you're missing a few tricks because you're too narrow in your thinking. So events this month can also offer a deeper appreciation of where your attention should be focused and how to positivity embrace change even when it's not what you want, as resisting means losing am opportunity.

Often being generous, not only financially, but also with the use of your talents and wisdom or experience can make such a difference, not only in the lives of others but in helping you reconnect with people who you usually feel apart from. This month is about giving of yourself to others and thus experiencing less separateness and more acceptance from people beyond your usual circles.

This is a time when you may lose the battle, but you are still winning the war, so it's important not to take a short-term view. Sometimes it's better to take a step back right now and strengthen your position in the long run. Even if you are in power struggle where your feel you are getting the rough end of the stick, that doesn't mean you can't learn from it and turn the tables at a later date.

In some cases you must make sure that you are not unconsciously giving out the single that you are going to be allowing yourself to be treated in some specific way. Human beings are creatures of habit, and often react in an instinctive way, so if you project to someone that a certain type of behavior is acceptable, they will keep doing it, they won't even think about it, and they won't self-correct. So this month it's all about boundaries, which is something you need to think about and impose longer term.

Marriage and Family

This can be an excellent opportunity to learn and deepen relationships. Even if there's some confrontation, you must analyze what an argument can teach you about something in your relationship? You must seek to foster communication or sharing that would have otherwise remained latent or unexpressed.

Your protective nature is in evidence and you really want what's best for the family, however you don't always go about it in the right way for example, you may seek greater control in all that you, your partner or children do, and you may seem overbearing as you could can insist on your way or the highway, as you've not in a compromising mood.

You have strong convictions, which although somewhat reassuring can rub family up the wrong way and so you need to know when to step back and allow others to adjust in their own time and manner.

You can sometimes seem oblivious to the concerns of those around you, but you're simply focusing on things in a different way and you don't always communicate that properly. You can be an effective leader in family matters as long as you're diplomatic not dogmatic or that just stirs up anger.

In marriage, it's very important to work on your boundaries, to know your own limits and to be able to define those limits in your own mind. Very often relationships run into to difficulty because the individuals have not examined in their own mind where their boundaries are and therefore they don't enforce them. So good relationships start with good boundaries, but good boundaries start with you having an internal conversation in your head about where your red lines are, and what you will and won't accept.

Money and Finance

This month there are ups and downs, and it's important for you to understand that not all is lost. This month is about recognizing what's not working, but also not overlooking what is still salvageable, and what has survived or been learned.

It's important for you to recognize new seeds of hope and growth and how you can nurture these.

Saturn retrograde in Pisces means that you have to be careful to fulfill contractual obligations and also see that other parties do likewise, because right now not everyone is talking the talk but not walking the walk.

Living and Loving to the Full

The key to relationship success this month is for you and your partner to set an 'intention', it doesn't necessarily have to be a date night or special event, it just has to be a set time for the relationship to be prioritized. Make sure that the date is in the diary and the kids are going to be with the grandparents or friends and work is going to be set aside. The good thing about planning a time without an agenda is that neither you nor your partner will develop any negative ideas about the time itself because what you're doing with that time isn't arranged, however you can agree not to talk about the kids, family, work or anything stressful.

When the time arrives you should go with the mood of the moment and use it as an opportunity to connect, it's so easy to lose connection in a relationship, so merely setting this intention to spend time together free from distractions helps you and a partner to get to know each other again and to have a forum to say things that usually never find time to be said.

Planetary Cautions

This may not be the best month for new sales initiatives, launching a website or short distance travel. It's important to understand fine print and details and to ensure people are all on the same page.

You've very self-motivated and individualistic this month, but you still need to be cooperative and working with others is inevitable. Even if it's time consuming or frustrating, you have to work with others and be as diplomatic as possible.

Moon Magic

The new moon phase extends from the 17th of July to the 30th of July this waxing phase is the perfect fortnight for new initiatives, setting plans, establishing goals, starting anything prospective and being proactive. This is the action phase, details below:

The waxing phase is great for networking, mixing business with pleasure, new platonic friendships or getting advice from friends. Political and humanitarian affairs are successful. Attending large scale events is favored. A great time for new social media campaigns.

The waxing phase is not ideal for new loans or taking on debt. Managing large sums of money is not advisable. Not a suitable time for tax and accounting changes.

Brand new activities and physical contact sports are not favored. You should be careful of diet, health and avoid extreme physical exertion.

AUGUST

***Essence and Energies – "I deal my own deck
Sometimes the ace, sometimes the deuces"***

The powerful energy this month is broadening your horizons, embracing what is unfamiliar and being willing to hobnob or interact with people from vastly different backgrounds.

It's important for you to seek information in new places, so whether it be in your job or in your hobbies, it's time to go about things a little bit differently, and to embrace more unorthodox approaches, because this can give you the edge.

This is not a time for rituals or structure, it's a time when you need to find a space in your life to live in the spirit of the moment. In many cases doing activities that are quite outdoorsy can give you a little bit of a rush, so this is a great time to do sports or outdoor activities that have a daring nature to them, where you challenge yourself a little bit and take on something that can get the adrenaline pumping.

The other energy that's important right now is leadership in terms of projects that are not directly connected to hobbies or your career. So it's a case of finding a cause or a problem, maybe something in your local neighborhood or community, and then being the one to step up find a solution and get other people inspired. So this is not a time to sit around waiting for things to get better, or waiting for things to change, it's time for you to be the change you want to see in your world, and you can actually do that in a very small way to begin with.

So the message is positive action that will encourage and inspire others, rather than simply identifying problems and complaining.

Affirmation: "Positive change in the world begins with me."

Love and Romance

Honesty is needed, as is a cold light of day assessment of your ongoing romances. Are you hanging onto a relationship that is emotionally jarring and no longer helping either of you thrive as individuals? Often there is a misguided sense of loyalty that's stopping you doing what needs to be done. It's time to diplomatically and discreetly withdraw from romances that have faded or become too contentious.

However, while some relationships must be let go, a good relationship that's in the doldrums can also be revived. It's possible that during this phase you hook up with an ex and because you and the ex-have now dealt with their issues and grown up, there is a viable second shot at the relationship.

Success in rescuing relationships this month is all about the extent to which you and a partner can take responsibility for your own problems and tackle them, without projecting them into the relationship or being blinkered to the extent of the problem.

Career and Aspiration

This is an ideal month for getting ahead and achieving both concrete goals and respect. You can get new projects off the ground fast and you can also make strides in terms of career land marks and impressing people who count.

You've both plucky and determined and your actions now tend to have long term consequences. Mars in your solar ninth house represent competition and so this month is ideal to compete in sports or to compete academically in terms of exams in higher education. An ideal time to impress others with your ideas and intellectual prowess.

Your words have more weight and carry greater power and you can increase your influence or spread ideas. You have a greater sense of the bigger picture and where your unique part in that picture is. This month is about being brave and also sticking to your principles, there is no success without a sense of truth and justice and you must uphold universal principles in all you do.

Adventure and Motivation

This month is ripe with positive energy and abundance and you need to use
it, although not necessarily all within the external world. The benefit of the
energies this month are often revealed as inner strength, confidence or
sense of purpose that can sustain you no matter what practical
circumstances demand of you.

In terms of ongoing activities which are already inspiration or going well,
this is the time to reinforce the best of what you're doing. If there are
obstacles which you're struggling with, then you must seek a quiet peace
that allows you to maintain an inner faith despite the hurdles or setbacks.

Your mind set is important as you've the capacity to draw benefits into
your life. Often past efforts can bring fulfillment, but you are unlikely to
take bold initiatives now.

Seeking alternative ways to improve yourself can bring significant results,
but often hurdles are the catalyst, whereas success doesn't necessarily lead
to the impetus for this improvement.

Marriage and Family

This month is an important one in marriage and while what passes between
you and your partner could be dramatic, subtle or both, a lot of what
happens will determine the future of the relationship and so you and your
partner should pay attention and be emotionally alert and adaptable.

It's likely that you or your partner will internally feel a strong resistance to
change when it comes to your approach and attitude to the relationship,
this stems from an insecurity and is totally understandable. However, for
marriage to thrive this month, you both have to deal with this insecurity
and not let it stop you from making the necessary adjustments in the
marriage.

You and your partner have to move out of comfort zones and risk
disagreements or disharmony for the sake of initiating change and getting
into a new groove that's ultimately going to serve both your interests better.

The biggest problem in love is believing that nothing can change or get better, because this attitude keeps you guys stuck in a place where neither of you can grow and it's like a prison.

It's very important for you and your partner to indulge each other, treat each other and spend quality time together, however it's not necessarily the conversation that's important, it's the ambience, the experience, the affection and escapism. So when you think ahead about how to spend time together to revitalize the romantic or sexual side of your relationship, you should be thinking about doing things that are creative like attending movies, music events, theatre etc. which can get you into the right frame of mind and encourage escapism as you sexual juices begin to flow. However, you also want to be thinking of changing up the way you relate to each other in the bedroom, you could do something like redecorating the bedroom, introducing new fabrics, making better use of music to put you in touch with that nostalgic side of yourself, even using sex toys and props can be helpful.

It's incredibly true that all work and no play makes us all dull, and adult life is full of pressure, stress, responsibility etc. and we do become very jaded and that leads to unimaginative love making or no lovemaking at all. So what's important this month is having pleasurable experiences with your partner that can remind you of who you really are is two unique, vibrant people who were once very much in love, but who possibly have become very tired out and broken through life.

Money and Finance

Nothing is cut and dried this month and even if you thought something was over, there may be a chance to go back over the old ground, find something new to chew over and perhaps with more investigation and discussion a new outcome can be reached. Old plans and projects still have life in them yet and you just need to apply a little magic. This is a very important month for deliberation and discussion, much of your time will be spent haggling over details and looking for compromises.

Although Capricorn are not great fence sitters, that is precisely what you need to do, you should be impartial. Your good judgment will be relied upon and you must be fair and just in the way you deal with finances and debtors.

Venus is retrograde in Leo this month, which indicates that you do need to be quite cautious in terms of joint financial ventures. It's not the best month to go in with other people to make an investment or plan a project, simply because it may be rather difficult to streamline your needs and your expectations with other people in the group.

This is a good time to get extra advice on things like inheritance tax, tax in general or insurance, you may simply not have all the necessary skills or understanding needed and getting some advice can be extremely reassuring.

Living and Loving to the Full

This month relationships need space. The best way to enhance a relationship is for you and your partner to go off and pursue an activity that fulfils and excites them individually and then come together again and share what you have experienced.

It's important to acknowledge where you both feel trapped or restricted in the relationship and thus to change your routines, so that you can both explore and discover things about yourselves separately.

Relationships are stronger when both parties are strong individuals, so both of your individuality needs a space to express itself.

Planetary Cautions

This month treading the middle ground and staying calm is vital. You must avoid any extreme reactions or jumping the gun.

You must avoid being drawn into conflict that is not your own and you should steer clear of taking sides in any arguments. You should not make decisions in the heat of the moment, it's a febrile atmosphere this month and emotions run high which is why it's easy to leap to conclusions, but things are changing so fast that that's not an option you choose. It's important to resist manipulation and pressure and you must be aware of what's real and what's propaganda.

Mercury retrograde from the 24th means that international travel, publishing and higher education goals can experience delay or disappointment. This is not a great time for advertising and promotional campaigns.

Moon Magic

The new moon phase extends from the 16th of August to the 30th of August this waxing phase is the perfect fortnight for new initiatives, setting plans, establishing goals, starting anything prospective and being proactive. This is the action phase, details below:

The waxing phase is not ideal for your promotional activities, competitive goals, higher education, publishing and team leadership. Not ideal for planning an important holiday. This phase is not suitable for publishing and advertising. Community goals and social work are not favored. Long distance travel is not favored.

An excellent month for marriage and engagement. Marriage counseling and initiatives to reignite understanding and cooperation in love are favored. Great for teamwork. A good time to choose new advisor ls or professional business partners. A favorable month for new romance and meeting potential partners. Creative and artistic ventures are successful. Great for launches and entertaining or throwing parties. Activities connected to children and young people are successful. Great for entering competitive arenas.

Suitable for investing and stock market activity. Analysis and problem solving is favored. Excellent for budgeting and organizing financial affairs.

Essence and Energies – "Don't be scared to fly alone
Find a path that is your own
Love will open every door
It's in your hands, the world is yours"

Now last month you didn't always feel in charge and sometimes you had to take a back seat, however this is an excellent month to do what you do best is lead, initiate and show others how it's done.

This is an excellent months for exercising your authority, it's important for you to show leadership in whatever work you do, and if you are the boss or run your own business, this is an excellent time to be a little bit more assertive about the direction your business is going in.

The key this month is starting it with your mission statement: you should be very specific about the goals you want to achieve this month, both in terms of career advancement but also in terms of your personal direction and where you feel your life should be heading. Then I'd like you to make a list, the list should be divided into aspiration and desire, which would incorporate your highest aims and wishes. Then I would like you to make another list of practical steps, and it doesn't matter how small these are as long as they steer you along the right route, and then I want you to write a list of what you feel is either scary, exciting or intimidating about these new goals and where you feel most confident.

Setting out your stall, making a stand and being ambitious isn't just about being confident and racing forward, it's about acknowledging any weaknesses you have and incorporating that into the game plan, but not letting the weaknesses hold you back.

Affirmation: "I have confidence in myself however I'm always willing to learn and I'm receptive to new information and learning."

Love and Romance

Now while romance was very much on the cards last month, and while Jupiter in your fifth house has created many opportunities, Jupiter turns retrograde this month in Taurus so it's time to evaluate new relationships. It's not necessarily a time to take a step back, but it's certainly a time to be realistic and to understand what they have to offer you and what their long-term potential will be.

This is often a time when there are logistical problems in relationships, perhaps travel issues, work related issues or family matters which keep you apart. These are all stumbling blocks for relationships in the medium term, as you have to figure out the best way forward and for Capricorn, often the only way is to be philosophical. The problems won't necessarily be worked out overnight, but you don't need to throw the relationship away, it's time to remain positive, to keep moving forward and importantly to keep enjoying the positives.

This is a tense and yet exciting month, and I do not think you will be getting much sleep. You are running on high octane, and it can be hard to switch off; you are quite excitable and spontaneous. Your desire to expand yourself regarding making new friends, learning and investing in your education and self-promotion can leave you a little stretched as you are initiating many new things and perhaps not giving all of them the attention they need to make them successful. So, you may want to spend more time focusing on the most important things rather than spreading yourself too thinly; you are not good right now at discerning what are the most important priorities you need to get to your goals.

So take a step back and think – this month you can get carried away in the flow, so much so that you get dizzy and lose your orientation. Others can also sway you off your course with their (often bad) ideas, and so stick with what you know. This month you are inspired to change tactics and use exciting new methods; however, this can be a gamble, and so you need to hedge your bets by not throwing away eve

Career and Aspiration

Mars is bringing a dynamic energy to your work life and no matter how high the work pile or what you have to face in terms of challenges, you have an inner confidence that thing are on the up and you will soon get to grips with things.

You're quite optimistic and your attitude is that of a winner, which is why you will attract that little extra bit of luck. You have an inner peace as you sense you'e doing the right thing and many of your recent decisions will be vindicated.

This a great time for establishing links abroad regarding new customers, new suppliers or even collaborating with fellow professionals in other parts of the world. It is an excellent time to learn from business practices in other countries, how to avoid their mistakes and use what works. Capricorn can make use of global trade agreements to forge ahead internationally.

Adventure and Motivation

With Venus now direct in Leo from the 4th, you are lucky in terms of competitions and also in your ability to win people over or influence an audience – if you have to give a speech or presentation you may get some very positive feedback, possibly negative too, but that is down to the power of what you have to say. The nail that stands proud gets hit first and so you can attract both acclaim and some criticism, but the important thing is that you've getting a message across. Remember the old adage, "There is no such thing as bad publicity".

You need to come to terms with both inner and outer manifestations of change. Subtle changes in attitude have a marked impact in focus and life direction. Often your spiritual and heart driven desires override the appeal of money, status and recognition and this can strongly impact on your choice of career or career focus going forward.

This month, the activation of Neptune definitely increases your spiritual awareness and you are more concerned about your sense of purpose and this leads to many of your preconceived ideas and notions washing away so that you can actually broaden your thinking and approach things from a different perspective.

This is the time to tune into your innermost depths, to take time for reflection. This is also not a time to self-censor, it's a time to explore the full range of emotions on the spectrum and incorporate them all into the wholeness of your being. This is a time to be honest about things you are inclined to deny, whether it's anger, bitterness or regret, and to bring anything that is buried to the forefront of your consciousness, so that you can think more clearly about it, embrace it and therefore create a healing space.

Marriage and Family

September is an excellent month to get clarity in relationships and to reaffirm commitment to each other and relationship goals. However it's also a time when you have to be patient about bridging the gap when there are big differences in your perception of the problems you face within your relationship or from the outside. Differences must be kept in proportion as not to cloud everything in the relationship.

Spiritual values matter to you in relationships, and those marriages which are founded on strong moral or religious values will thrive and can weather storms with love getting stronger. This is a tougher month for those relationships in which you both come from different religions or where one has a very different moral code. In these mixed religion/mixed value relationships, you guys will have to work harder to find common ground, especially in connection with bringing up the children, which can be a big bone of contention.

This is the time when you have to be quite careful with the way you handle your children you cannot be authoritarian or punitive, but at the same time you cannot let them get away with murder, so it's striking a clever balance where you allow them freedom but are clear that the must adhere to high principles.

Money and Finance

Venus direct in Leo from the 4th is excellent news for things resolving and moving forward financially. Problems with disagreements between you and business partners can be resolved. You may get good news about a loan or mortgage deal or you could be able to resolve debt issues. This is a good time to settle disputes about money with an ex-partner.

Passive income from subscriptions, royalties, benefits or donations again begins to flow, in other cases, these avenues can now be pursued.

Living and Loving to the Full

The key in enhancing love magic this month is for you and your partner to think about your relationship in the long term, the adventure that you are having together and the sense of shared experience. It's good to look back on what you've been through together, the laughter, the tears, the triumphs and the failures and see it all in context.

Enhancing love magic is all about acceptance and being able to release the negative while focusing on positive this should not be a time of finger pointing or accusations, it should be a time of understanding your relationship in the context of your life journey and appreciating what you have brought to each other's lives.

Planetary Cautions

During the Mercury retrograde period, Mercury is in your ninth house and so this is a period when you can have a mini crisis in terms of your confidence in your direction. You can be quite unpredictable, you are restless and may even appear to be having a mini midlife crisis. You are attracted to instant gratification and may act recklessly. You can be overconfident and may bite of more than you can chew. A partner should take anything you say with a pinch of salt as you tend to exaggerate or embellish. You don't always have a good grip of reality, although you can have sudden insights which are quite inspirational.

You probably won't keep promises and you're likely to let people down as you get carried away with whims and often do not keep up with what you've been saying. You're often quite exciting to be with during this phase as you're ready to consider anything, however you've also rather distracted and it's hard to hold your attention and have important conversations.

Moon Magic

The new moon phase extends from the 14th of September to the 29th of September this waxing phase is the perfect fortnight for new initiatives, setting plans, establishing goals, starting anything prospective and being proactive. This is the action phase, details below:

The waxing phase is great for dating, new relationships and your social life. This period is ideal for date nights, attending sporting and leisure events or theatre. It's an excellent time to pursue creative and artistic ventures for business and pleasure. Activities with children, both your own and within your work are successful. New jobs or business connected to children are favored. This is a good waxing period for fun, but also for problem solving and new innovative solutions in your work and personal life.

A good phase for spiritual awareness, meditation, spiritual goals or retreats. An excellent time to deal with large corporate entities or government departments. New work in the charitable or rehabilitation sector is successful. Great for highly inspirational and artistic goals. Private space is important, as is reflection. Music and poetry writing is successful. This isn't a good time to arrange trips, travel overseas or make long term decisions as things will crop up to disrupt your/his plans.

You've more likely to question recent decisions you've made and it's not the best time to make you commit to anything.

***Essence and Energies - "And we can build this dream together
Standing strong forever
Nothing's gonna stop us now"***

This month the essence is grit and determination, it's about sticking with a task, seeing it through the end and not been deterred by obstacles. This is a time to use the sheer force of will and to gain strength by struggling against all odds and succeeding.

This may be a great month to pick something particularly intimidating or arduous to do whether it be a mental or physical task, and to use your Capricorn powers of concentration and determination to pull off a result.

This is an excellent month for activities that need a lot of stamina and therefore it's a perfect time for any sporting quest that you have been training for, alternatively this is a great time to begin training for a marathon, triathlon or setting yourself a particularly daunting task that will bring you a lot of satisfaction and greater levels of strength or fitness.

This is also great for nonphysical tasks that are connected to things that you usually put off for another day simply because they are not so appealing, but this is a good time to get yourself thoroughly stuck into something it's a little bit difficult and requires focus, because you can nail it, and it will boost your confidence knowing that you overcame that hurdle.

Affirmation: "Nothing can stop me when I put my mind to something."

Love and Romance

You are likely to be in a very amorous mood and if you're single, you're more likely to relate positively and give off the right chemistry to members of the opposite sex, making this a time when you are likely to attract a new partner into your life.

This is a good time for dating and meeting potential partners and a rather passionate and exciting relationship can result, but one of the downsides is you are more likely to have your jealousy and envy aroused, and your relationships can contain a certain element of competition where there's a bit of love-hate going on. One minute you may feel excited and rather inspired by your partner, but the next moment he/she may be triggering you or causing you concern because of his/her flirting.

This month is a rather complicated one for romantic relationships, relationships started now can become very intense, but also quite draining. You may be in for more than you bargained for in love, as while new relationships may feel like they are meant to be, they will not be easy and may come with heavy responsibility.

New relationships often have issues with control and power and you can find yourself getting drawn into deeply manipulative situations. You need to have a taste for drama in love if you are to embark on a relationship this month, as it will be tense and demanding, even though it can also offer fulfilment if you are seeking a very committed and serious relationship.

Career and Aspiration

A sense of purpose and a connection with your own integrity can be your lantern as you enter somewhat of a metaphorical dark cave, where you will deal with some formidable forces. Your opponents this month are resolute and determined, they are also cunning and so you have to stay on your toes and be ready for anything. Just as your lantern can only cast light a certain distance in this dark cave, you can only go a few steps at a time, as you cannot see far enough ahead to fully appreciate what is next. You have to use your Capricorn common sense, but also your sense of adventure to deal with this month and be patient, but also intrepid.

You must try not to be fanatical, you can get carried away and may get involved in either office politics or other matters that are really none of your business and in which you may stir the pot rather than helping to resolve anything.

This is an excellent time for planning in terms of your professional life or your immediate future. It's a very good time to schedule, to brainstorm, to strategize and to lay out plans so that you have a good basis to work from to achieve things that will increase your chances of success and better opportunities.

This is a wonderful time to fire off résumés to prospective employers, it's also a good time to totally rewrite your resume and revamp all your professional and social media profiles, so that they all look slick, appealing and bang up to date.

This can also be a good time to attend a training course related to your profession, and it's also wise to go to seminars and conferences where you have a chance to make speeches or be seen by people in your professional community, so that you can be a breast of opportunities available.

Adventure and Motivation

The best use of your energy is in motivating teams and helping those you works with to achieve goals or targets which have already been set rather than suddenly changing the goal posts or coming up with brand new directions. It's tempting for you to play the joker this month, but while you should use humor to lighten the mood within your workmate, you must be careful that the joke does not end up being on you.

You must take control over the way you approache your artistic work and be less haphazard. It could be time to be more businesslike about your hobbies – often hobbies are so important to self-actualization and expression that they deserve more time and more seriousness to get more from the process and achieve your ambitions in that direction. So you should have a schedule, and devote more time, enter competitions or attend workshops – be more daring in the way you develop your artistic talents. You can turn hobbies into business opportunities, but you first need to be more serious.

Marriage and Family

Criticism in love can hurt this month, and yet you should pay attention to it as it may be meant more kindly than you have perceived it – so you should not let a small rebuff turn into a cold war. The danger this month is that fairly banal or mundane comments can give rise to reactions that are disproportionate and which damage the love vibe – you have the power here, your reactions if measured and balanced can rescue any situation and take things forward. However, if you throws the baby out with the bathwater, it can be hard work to get things back to where they were.

In all love matters, you should take a deep breath, breathe, and count to 20 or maybe even 50. It can often be that what hits a nerve is when you hear your own fears or insecurities echoed back at you via things your partner says – it is then that you see red. What you may be missing is that a partner is trying to help you not be critical for criticism's case.

In marriages and also in new relationships, children can create obstacles, and this is especially true for blended families with step-children and also where couples get together later in life and have to split time between romance and other commitments.

Money and Finance

There are hiccoughs and U-Turns regarding your financial plans or investment decisions for the next few months, and it is back to the drawing board to refine and perfect. Sometimes months like that happen to make you realize that what you thought was adequate actually was not your best and a second stab at something is needed.

There is a great need for focus and discipline, especially for creative work and management decisions, whether that is hobby, leisure or work-related.

Living and Loving to the Full

Enhancing love magic is about sharing and emotional expression without coming over as needy.

You are very compassionate and generous when your romantic feelings are aroused; however you have to be careful that you do not give too much away too quickly. You're quick to open up in new love relationships, and yet you may be overeager and may reveal your hand too soon or even come over as needy or oversharing. In fact, you're not needy at all, you've just excited about sharing deep feelings, as talking to someone special and opening up about your past or deeper emotions just feels right and good, and you get a lot from it; you just need to be certain you are doing it with a person you can really trust, as some things are not really fit for the ears of strangers. You must also be careful that you do not attract someone who has more problems than you are really able to deal with.

This is a time when you likely to be attracted to someone who is fairly popular and good-looking, and while you are physically aroused by them, it may be a challenge when this person flirts or has a wide circle of friends, because you may question their attachment to yourself. So you have to be quite secure within yourself when you're dating right now, if you are feeling a little bit fragile and vulnerable, you are likely to feel easily rebuffed or rejected, meaning it can be tricky dating right now.

Planetary Cautions

It's important for you to find the middle ground, it's all too easy for you to be tempted into extreme approaches, but these will simply alienate others.

You must resist pressure even if it's intense and you should keep your focus. The more mature you are and the more you know yourself, the better this month proceeds, however a lack of self-awareness or properly thought through goals will inevitably lead to you falling into traps or being manipulated by others.

You must keep your head about you when others are losing theirs. You must be alert but not reactionary. You must fence sit rather than rush headlong in any particular direction.

Moon Magic

The new moon phase extends from the 14th of October to the 28th of October this waxing phase is the perfect fortnight for new initiatives, setting plans, establishing goals, starting anything prospective and being proactive. This is the action phase, details below:

In the waxing phase it's excellent for financial analysis and business decisions. Getting promotion or achieving a pay rise or greater sales is favored. Good for better cash flow, investing and buying new assets. A good time for purchasing and expanding a business.

You should be cautious in getting advice, employing a consultant, legal battles, asset management, financial audits and tax affairs.

New sexual relationships aren't favored.

Essence and Energies – "Brass in pocket."

This month it's time to exercise your individuality, you should embrace change and you should express yourself in your own unique and innovative way. It's important to make a stand about who you really are, and you should follow your heart and your integrity.

What's important about this month is breaking away from restrictions or burdens that no longer fulfil you or fit in with your life plan. This can be a time when you suddenly make a radical change or break from the past and this can be very good for you.

Don't be afraid to do the unexpected, rebel against things that contain you and stifle you.

This is a good time for a sudden lifestyle change that can radically impact your health for the better. It's important right now to reimagine your future, and to grab onto those hopes and dreams that are slipping away, don't give up on yourself and don't give up on your future.

Affirmation: "Life is for living and I resolve to live my best life fearlessly expressing myself and following my star."

Love and Romance

This month can often be characterized by a bolt from the blue, something totally unexpected that happens in your relationship or love life. You may experience a lucky chance where there is a changing in your fortunes, there may be a sudden opportunity that significantly changes either your love life or your attitude to romance in general.

This is certainly a time where you should rule nothing out, be spontaneous, adventurous and see where it takes you.

Romance, new and established, is favored. You are more diplomatic and easygoing, which means you let small things lie and concentrate on the good things, promoting well-being and congeniality between you and a partner.

Going out and attending theatre, movies, concerts are something you and a partner should be doing often, and for established couples, it is time you rediscovered that side of life. It is important to get out and enjoy yourselves together in activities that transport you away from yourselves into a fantasy world and which inspire the imagination.

Films or even porn (if that is what you guys enjoy) can enhance or stimulate the sex life, and more than that, can help open the door to conversations about sex, new things to try or what you may both enjoy.

Being in love can make you spendthrift, so you should not allow romantic vibes to deplete your bank account with too many impulse purchases.

Career and Aspiration

Your confidence and self-esteem can face a challenge this month – but this is merely a call for you to handle yourself in a slightly different way and should be seen as an opportunity improvement, especially in the way you deal with those in authority or conduct yourself in the public arena.

You must be a little guarded and should pick the subjects about which you talk carefully, ensuring that you keeps your options open. Words are powerful, and so you must ensure you use them in a way that drives the point home without opening the door for you to be pigeon holed or locked into a blind alley. You must stay on message, and not be drawn into arguments or debates that are not central to the issue. Distractions can often cause you to go off on a tangent and miss opportunities to reach an audience.

This is an excellent month for growth and expansion, now the year is winding down and lot of people are already checking out and waiting to next year, but for Capricorn that would be a lost opportunity, because this is definitely a month when opportunities will present themselves for learning, travelling and gaining valuable new experiences. So rather than closing down the year, and stopping trying anything because of the coming holidays, you can rather begin to broaden, expand and there can be some unexpected surprises and treasures.

It's very possible that you will be handed a brand new project to deal with, and this will incorporate both elements within and without your experience, so there's a steep learning curve, some challenges, however what is possible, is a great deal of satisfaction and the opportunity to impress either the public or your superiors.

Adventure and Motivation

You're more pioneering and this month will be inclined to explore and visit places within your vicinity which offer new experiences and a taste of the exotic or even esoteric. You're more open right now, and your expansiveness could include reading materials which you would normally not bother with, but which offer new insights. You're drawn to what's obscure and off the beaten track for adventure.

Friends may lend you book or drag you off to see arty films or perhaps invite you to an event which ends up being quite a culturally interesting experience. Your ability to communicate is enhanced, and you can use this time to promote your ideas or lend intellectual support to campaigns you care about. It is a time of action mentally, where you look to increase knowledge and then distribute that knowledge to others. This is an exciting month when you will feel positive and optimistic and even challenging tasks or problems will be taken on with a 'can do' attitude.

Marriage and Family

You and your partner may both feel like being more social, more experimental and like doing some liberating activities this month. It is a great time for throwing off the shackles and embarking on a mini adventure – i.e. you may both join a new sports club, you may start arranging a cultural trip, you may begin learning a language together or attend mass event that really inspires you both or join a political party – the theme is that you and your partner will begin a journey together linked to invigorating hopes, dreams and aspirations.

Relationships are all about growing together spiritually, and so any love relationship is enhanced where you guyhs have similar dreams and where these hopes are bigger than yourselves (i.e. political or social goals) or mundane material issues.

This may not be a time to get obsessed with the rights or wrongs of and situation, just go with it. The key in love and romance is risk, take a chance, forget your rulebook.

November is about looking to change the way your relationships work. You are much more interested in asserting control and that doesn't mean that you necessarily want to control your partner, but you may want to challenge the norms of your relationship. You may be a lost lot less compromising and you could be more difficult to work with. You have a greater sense of your own individuality, which can be a little bit of a problem for relationships where you had become too tied up in 'being a couple' and had possibly felt that you had lost yourself.

Money and Finance

Quickly arranged business trips can be very successful even if they are highly speculative. Understanding that perception is often more important than reality is essential when understanding your clients, fellow professionals or the public.

Often people begin to feel something, and though they may not be able to rationally say why they feel that way or provide facts, it can be very hard to shift a perception once it settles in, and so if you need to work with the public, you must try and understand their perceptions and acknowledge them. If you ignore them, you can miss opportunities to connect with money making opportunities.

The political environment both this month and this year is very much one of rebellion, change, and displeasure with the way things are – there is a wave of rebellion and distrust growing, and Capricorn who find ways to tap into that, or work with that can be very successful.

Living and Loving to the Full

An excellent time for a weekend away or surprise trip organized by you or your romantic partner.

The good vibes must be given an opportunity to flow in love, and the only downside in love is if your partner is feeling very down and not sharing your enthusiasm. If your partner is down or negative, it could be within your gift to inject them with some of your positivity, which is in abundance.

You must use your PMA to help your partner see some solutions and help lift their spirits and get them out of their own bubble of gloom. If you've in a situation where your partner's issues and problems are so pervasive that they are bringing you down, you need to mentally and emotionally detach from them, not in a selfish way, but in a self-preserving way so that you conserves and makes the most of your own positivity this month

Planetary Cautions

Basically, you should not go along with anything old fashioned, closed minded or hackneyed and then use that as an excuse for failure. The key is to stick with what you believe, but not to be conservative, you must adapt and innovate.

You should not be scared to disrupt the status quo as even if you're in a minority of one you can still be right, as although you may be unpopular in the short run, you can be vindicated and avoid the folly of the mainstream with superior wisdom.

Protecting valuables is essential. Insurance is good, but you must also take steps to protect electronic data and use registered mail to send important documents.

Moon Magic

The new moon phase extends from the 13th of November to the 27th of November this waxing phase is the perfect fortnight for new initiatives, setting plans, establishing goals, starting anything prospective and being proactive. This is the action phase, details below:

The waxing phase is not great for investing and buying assets. You need to be more cautious with money. It may be harder to start a new business venture or money making scheme. It's best to stick with what you know. Lack of information makes it hard for you to make financial decisions. You should stay flexible financially and avoid increasing costs.

This is not a suitable time for marriage or engagement. Marriage counselling is not successful in that waxing phase. New business associations should not be initiated. This is not a good time to employ a new advisor.

This favors legal matters, negotiation, diplomacy and making deals connected to import export. It's favorable for sporting events or community fund raising. Ideal for academic goals and further education. Business expansion to new geographical areas, advertising, promotion and publishing is successful.

The waxing phase is not a successful time for new business ventures, business investment or assets purchases. A major sales push us not advisable. This is not a good time to buy previous metals, crypto or trade in Forex.

Essence and Energies – "Write the songs that make the whole world sing."

This is an excellent month for the aesthetic side of life and it's wonderful to explore your emotions through the use of art or music.

Artistically you should pursue your music or your writing with greater urgency as you feel this need to get something within yourself out, you need to express an energy and often you do this most effectively via music or art.

December is a month of labors of love – a time when you are happy to put in extra effort or even conduct laborious thankless work because something matters to you on a higher level. Material values are less important and spiritual matters perhaps disguised as creative, or humanitarian pursuits will take precedence. Often you experience the divine via hobbies and interests which you follow, and even if you are not religious, you will have a greater sense of the interconnectivity of life and the special meaning behind events.

ESP and psychic feelings are stronger, and you may also have a strong sense of family members who have died – you may feel their presence more than usual or see them in dream in a positive and supportive way.

Affirmation: "I am open to receiving inspiration from the higher realms of existence."

Love and Romance

Some frustration and challenge is to be expected on a personal level. It's often a time of misunderstandings in relationships, probably because you guys are both being less objective or are confused. In fact, you and your partner are probably giving each other mixed messages, so therefore you guys have to try hard to communicate clearly or give each other space.

An excellent time to meet new partners, however you may not connect romantically right away, you may exchange numbers and communication begins rather slowly at first. It's not that you're reticent about love, but you are very busy and romance may not come top of your list.

You may find you begin new friendships which others see as ill-advised – it may seem like a new group or person has a hold over you and is leading you astray.

If you think something holds the answers then you will go against what you have always known or believed and even against your own immediate interests. All this has a purpose, you are looking to find out which patterns of behavior or thought are holding you back and the only way you can do that is by throwing your 'rule book' out the window and going with a whole new flow to see what sets you free and opens up new avenues.

Career and Aspiration

This is an excellent time for work which requires focus, concentration, mental stamina and determination. It suits you if you're studying, memorizing facts and trying to achieve a greater knowledge in technical fields. It is a time when you are able to be serious, business like, hard headed and rational, it certainly assists you in your business decisions and your work life as your thinking is clear and factual.

This is not necessarily a time where you learn quickly, but what you do learn you will learn well, and it will stay with you. If you're currently struggling to master a new skill or area of knowledge, this will give you the patience and mental perseverance to get on top of your studies.

During this time you may have significant communications with other people: you may have to deal with bureaucracy, fill in important forms, make claims, give testimony, compile information for a lawsuit or an important application. It is more likely that you will have dealings with government and officials, and it's important to take an organized systematic approach to your paperwork.

Adventure and Motivation

This month supercharges your ability to be effective in working with images i.e. photography, cinematography and also positive visualisation.

You may also be drawn to water sports, the ocean or activities involving the great outdoors. There is a desire to escape and be free or to revel in a fantasy world looking for distractions.

This is a dreamy time that fosters creativity in the arts and dance. It can be a phase where you procrastinates or put off anything difficult or stressful.

You are able to inspire others with your ideas and you can succeed in any teaching or mentoring role. You enjoy talking about concepts, but you have the ability to rationalize these and bring them into the practical realm.

Marriage and Family

In relationships you're eager to get answers, to have honest exchanges and to rationally iron out problems. It's a time when you don't put things off in relationships, you will be eager to have difficult conversations and progress can definitely be made.

Marriage relations improve if you're open to listening and are more understanding of your partner's points of view, you should be ready to take new information on board and should do so objectively. You are less inclined to get emotional or become defensive, as you can see the logic of what your partner is conveying. However, you will not hold back on your own opinions either, and you can be tempted to take the moral high ground and assume a righteous approach, which you must try not to do. It's time to be positive and think of solutions, you should try not to get sidetracked into the rights and wrongs, not everything had a moral angle to it.

This can be a very tricky month for divorces regarding legalities and also in terms of one or both of you being difficult due to lingering hurt feelings – remember that often the cleaner the break, the better for both of you, and so know when to bury the hatchet and stop playing games. Ex-partners suddenly pitching up can disrupt new relationships or cause you to have mixed feelings; remember the only way is forward NOT back, and so remember why the previous relationship went wrong and do not expect a different result a second time.

Money and Finance

You tend to be more excitable right now and can jump the gun. You should avoid financial decisions as they may be made based on feelings, which are running high, rather than good financial data. Impulse control is lower and you may be a little spendthrift.

It's best for you not to sign a new contract this month, you need to stay flexible as changes to your circumstances are possible this month, which could render a new loan or contract useless or too onerous.

You shouldn't be dismayed if negotiations drag on, you should use the delay to go over the details once again and to truly understand any knock on effects.

Living and Loving to the Full

You should take the initiative in sexual and intimate matters, be more physical, use body language and affectionate physical closeness to turn your partner on. Capricorn is very visual in love this month, the package matters and so you are more likely to be turned off by a partner who is putting on weight and not looking after themselves. Improving your sex life may go hand in hand with encouraging your partner to get fit, be healthier and trim down or buying a partner sexy new lingerie/undewear.

Use of massage is important in sex to get the carnal juices flowing, however a good argument may also turn you on if it gets the heart pumping and the emotional blocks out of the way.

Planetary Cautions

You should be ambitious and follow your heart, but remember not to take on more than you can handle. It's important not to overreach yourself just to try and impress those in authority, you should remember it's more important to be true to yourself than to impress people externally.

Sometimes there are difficulties with other people, these usually come from false expectations, so it's important for you to go into any new relationships, both business and romantic, with a clearer idea of what everyone has to offer and the reality of the situation. You should be optimistic but still realistic.

Mercury goes retrograde on the 14th in Capricorn this can cause you to backtrack on certain plans and you may begin to doubt yourself. It's a period of teething problems and wondering if you have done the right thing, however you shouldn't turn the clock back, you must keep moving forward and use the next few weeks as a chance to refine your plans or make some readjustments. Your fundamental strategy and plans are sound, however you may need to tinker around the edges, put out a few fires, as it were, and sharpen up as the game may be slightly different now you are in it, to what you had imagined.

Moon Magic

The new moon phase extends from the 12th of December to the 26th of December this waxing phase is the perfect fortnight for new initiatives, setting plans, establishing goals, starting anything prospective and being proactive. This is the action phase, details below:

The waxing phase is not great for large scale financial reorganization, managing money for others or accounting goals. Negotiations about money can be fruitless. Getting married or engaged is not favored.

Mercury is retrograde in Capricorn from the 14th meaning that debating and presenting yourself or doing activities involving a great deal of communication can be tricky. This can be frustrating for travel, negotiations and discussion in love. Learning, writing and journalism need patience and attention to detail. You need to be precise and organized.

This is not the best time for highly competitive events, public speaking or debate.

This is a good time for dealing with large corporate entities and government bureaucracy. Charitable and humanitarian affairs are favored. This is also a great time for retreats, being alone or introspection. Spiritual matters are favored. A good time for new work involving water, the ocean, water sports or sailing.

Leadership, innovation, enterprise and new activities are favored. Good for artistic inspiration, performance and activities that require confidence. Suitable for competitive activities.

Great for using intuition, understanding dreams or working alone on artistic or musical goals. Good for writing romantic love letters.

A great waxing phase for new career directions, new business ventures and changes in life goals. Pioneering action, reputational improvement and being head hunted is possible. A time for major new initiatives in supercharging life direction. A great time for PR, job interviews and corporate entertainment.

A good period for love, finding love and dating. A good time to improve social relationships and enjoy parties and leisure activities. An excellent time to be affectionate, have date nights and show appreciation to a partner.

Excellent for new creative ventures and entertainment events and launches. Business and matters connected to children are favored.

Well that's a wrap of our biggest most comprehensive Capricorn Horoscope yet.

Whether you are a Capricorn or know a Capricorn, I do believe you will have found this very helpful and informative.

I aim to give you a variety of advice based on psychology, spiritual insight, relationship advice and business guidance, so you get a little bit of everything.

Take care and have a wonderful 2023.

Blessings, Lisa.

www.ingramcontent.com/pod-product-compliance
Lightning Source LLC
Chambersburg PA
CBHW071347130726
47996CB00002B/840